The Chemically Dependent Woman

R$_x$: Recognition
Referral
Rehabilitation

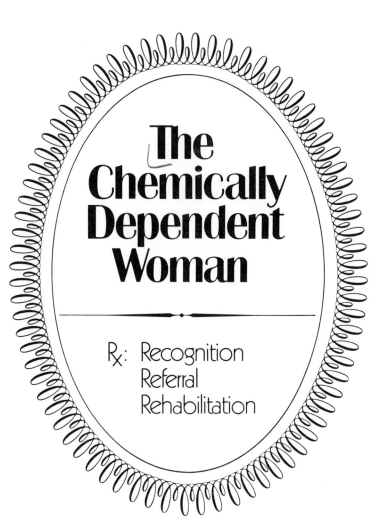

The Chemically Dependent Woman

Rx: Recognition
Referral
Rehabilitation

Edited by JANET DOWSLING and ANNE MacLENNAN

Proceedings of a Conference sponsored by the Donwood Institute, Toronto, June 4, 1977

Addiction Research Foundation
Toronto, Canada

I.S.B.N. 0-88868-026-0

Printed and bound in Canada

Contents

Introduction

Specialists in the chemical dependence field believe serious drinking problems among women are far more prevalent than any figures have yet shown and that most such problems remain unrecognized and untreated. Figures that do exist suggest that anywhere from one in six to one in three problem drinkers is a woman. Some even say the ratio is one to one.

In Ontario, as an example, this could mean that of 400,000 problem drinkers, as many as 200,000 may be women.

At the same time, more women are seeking help from physicians. Feeling obligated to "do something" for their patients, physicians tend to prescribe tranquillizers. The evidence increasingly suggests they do that too often.

In addition, doctors are often not aware patients may have an alcoholism problem. The result is that many women are becoming cross-addicted. At The Donwood Institute, 27% of female patients are cross-addicted.

To understand the changing and ever-increasing demands on physicians and therapists by women and their families, it is necessary to refresh and revitalize our thinking. What is the effect of the role of WOMAN in society that is helping to create these problems and how can we increase our skills in the early recognition, referral, and rehabilitation of the special health problems of women.

Traditionally, treatment for women has been viewed from a male vantage point. If treatment is carried out primarily by men, in a male-oriented society, it is tempting to conclude that current treatment therefore obviously fails to take into account special needs of women. It is particularly tempting in the field of addictions.

With this in mind, we felt a need for a seminar on the chemically dependent woman where the special issues of women in need of assistance would be discussed by women actively involved in dealing with women.

ACKNOWLEDGEMENTS

Thank you

To the staff of The Donwood Institute who formed the Seminar
Planning Committee:
    Doreen Birchmore, head of the day clinic;
    Janet Dowsling, physician;
    Rosemary McNaughton, director of patient care; and
    Heather Rowe, personnel and public relations officer.

To Douglas W. Macdonald, physician, executive director, and
clinical director of The Donwood, who acknowledged the
importance of holding the seminar on the chemically
dependent woman, and who supported and encouraged its
implementation.

To the Women's Counselling Referral and Education Center,
which assisted with early planning of the seminar.

THE DONWOOD INSTITUTE

The Donwood Institute represents the culmination of over thirty years experience in the treatment of addictive disorders. In 1946 and 1947, Dr. R.G. Bell began by treating alcoholic patients in his own home near Toronto. In 1948 the Shadowbrook Hospital for men and in 1951 the Willowdale Hospital for women were organized. The Bell Clinic, which combined the two, opened in 1954 and continued to operate an in-patient and out-patient service for both men and women until replaced by The Donwood Institute in March, 1967.

The Donwood Institute is a special public hospital for patients disabled by alcohol and drug dependence and the related problems. Its two year health and therapy plan is initiated by an intensive 28 day program of examination, instruction, counselling and therapy on both an in-patient and Day Clinic basis. The long-range objectives are to interrupt and inactivate dependence, to achieve optimal repair of the related physical, psychological and social problems, and to establish a new rewarding lifestyle based on sound health principles. Clinical, non-clinical and patient personnel combine to provide a supportive community during the transition period from the old lifestyle to a new one.

In addition to evaluation of results up to five years after initial treatment, Donwood is increasingly involved in educational and counselling services for families and training programs for outside clinical personnel.

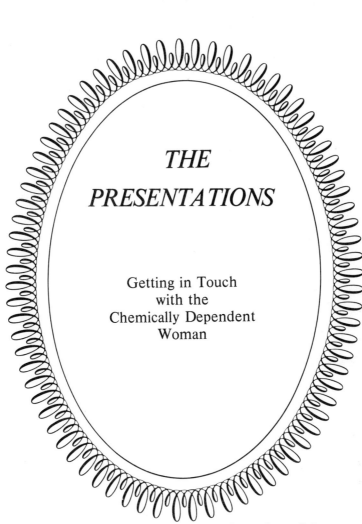

THE
PRESENTATIONS

Getting in Touch
with the
Chemically Dependent
Woman

The Chemically Dependent Woman: An Overview of the Problem

by R. Gordon Bell

Since I have been given the honor of introducing your seminar, I shall take this opportunity to summarize briefly my opinions on this topic, and conclude with a few suggestions for future action.

Within recent decades, we have witnessed a rapidly expanding awareness of the health hazards associated with the intake of a wide range of food and non-food substances. In the 1930s and 40s, this awareness was mainly focused on alcoholic beverages and opium derivatives. In the 1950s and 60s, it expanded to include concern about misuse of a wide variety of synthetic drugs: barbiturates and other sedatives, amphetamines and other stimulants, LSD and other hallucinogens, made alarming headlines before the hazards of the most popular of all prescription drugs—the benzodiazepine tranquillizers—were eventually recognized.

In spite of our fascination with the new synthetic products, all of the old-time biological derivatives—alcohol, heroin, marijuana, cocaine, nicotine, and caffeine—continued to increase in popularity and abuse. Finally, in the 1960s and 70s, an unprecedented expansion of interest and understanding in better nutrition began to initiate a counter trend to healthier

---

Dr Bell is founder and president of The Donwood Institute, Toronto.

intake habits. The point I wish to emphasize is that the progression of awareness of new health hazards during the middle third of the century has contributed to a gradation and fragmentation of clinical and community effort to cope with the related problems. It is my personal conviction that total intake habits should be considered as one unit in a comprehensive health program. To date, there has been a tendency in clinical and scientific circles to concentrate on a particular intake pattern, such as smoking or eating, with imbalanced attention to the others.

From new evidence concerning the relationship of total intake to health at all stages of the life process, from conception to death, I am convinced a new, more comprehensive orientation to this crucial health problem is required. At no time in the past have we been so threatened by multiple involvement with the world of chemicals. We are threatened, first, by self-administration of a bewildering variety of biological and synthetic products originally taken for their relaxing, stimulating, or awe-inspiring effects; second, by a still more mysterious assortment of chemicals administered by our industrialized community, as pollutants, food additives, or food preservatives. Finally, through food-processing, we often disturb the natural balance of nutrients required for optimal functioning of the human organism.

Nature of Addiction

The word addiction has been defined in so many ways that the term is practically useless. If I use the word, I am referring to a dependence on harmful quantities of one or more substances, that persists in spite of awareness of progressive damage to personal health, social relationships, or both. Harmful quantities refers to both the obvious rapid effects of acute intoxication, and the hidden, gradual, progressive damage of chronic intoxication. Whenever the experience of intoxication is pleasant or otherwise rewarding, the additional threat of dependence on the effects of harmful quantities has to be considered. When a controlled dependence on harmful quantities expands to an uncontrolled dependence, the unfortunate victim becomes locked into a lifestyle that has acute and chronic intoxication as the inevitable consequences. This is the condition commonly referred to as addiction.

An uncontrolled dependence on alcohol will be used to illustrate the progressive phases in dependence:

1) *Reactive Phase* The initial dependence on alcohol is a reaction to a personal desire for change, to a social situation, or to both. Unless harmful quantities are involved, no clinically significant situations develop.

2) *Habitual Phase* Recurrent reactive use eventually becomes habitual use and thus, a routine coping technique in an infinite variety of personal and social situations. The total intake of alcohol is directly related to the degree of habitual dependence. If the intake of alcohol is below the quantities capable of initiating cumulative physical and psychological effects for that individual, the habitual dependence phase may be maintained indefinitely with minimal risk to personal health or social relationships. On the other hand, if the intake, unwittingly or wittingly, involves the harmful quantities capable of producing undesirable, cumulative effects, sooner or later the drinker becomes aware of it. At this point, an expanding, habitual dependence on alcohol begins to expand still more by habitual defence of dependence.

3) *Defensive Phase* When a drinker reaches the point of having to defend his drinking, in spite of awareness of undesirable consequences, habitual dependence on alcohol has clearly grown to become the outstanding coping mechanism in day-to-day living. This is the stage at which the frightening power of a harmful dependence on alcohol or drugs begins to be evident to both victims and associates. Alibis, lying, cover-up, projection, resentment, manipulation, and preoccupation with supply, dominate the mental processes and progressively crowd concern for other activities and responsibilities out of consciousness.

4) *Helpless Phase* Eventually, a break in tolerance for alcohol heralds general breakdown in the capacity to cope with anything. All situations—at home, work, or elsewhere—are experienced as increasingly difficult and stressful. Since drinking has become the main coping mechanism, dependence accelerates as tolerance declines.

5) *Surrender Phase* The predicament of expanding dependence and declining tolerance will soon terminate in premature death, from accident, illness, or suicide; in total surrender to dependence with no attempt to maintain family, occupational, or community status; or, in a search for help. This was the condition originally referred to in the first step of Alcoholics Anonymous.

6) *Declining Phase* If help is found — in AA, clinics, or elsewhere — uninterrupted abstinence and thus, lack of reinforcement of dependence, results in a phase of declining dependence, over a period of from one to two years.

7) *Inactive Phase* Finally, a phase is reached when dependence has been reduced to the point that there is no longer any conscious awareness of missing alcohol. New coping mechanisms have been developed and stabilized by new habit patterns in all the personal and social situations that formerly demanded alcohol.

Clinical Programs

The decisions concerning care of chemically threatened or damaged people, should be based on consideration of both the basic common factors, and the special problems related to age, sex, profession, social status, and the particular products concerned. For example, the total lifestyle associated with gross abuse of the amphetamines, plus the cumulative damage from chronic amphetamine intoxication, produces a clinical problem that cannot be treated successfully at The Donwood Institute. The Donwood program involves bringing staff, patients, family, and other associates together to form a supplementary, supportive community for a two-year period of transition to a new and healthier lifestyle. The patient must be able to become involved effectively in this program in the relatively short period of from four to seven weeks. Most patients, of all ages and both sexes, who have developed a harmful dependence on alcohol, sedatives, tranquillizers, or narcotics, can graduate from the need of daily support to weekly support within that time, while the amphetamine addict may require a year to attain a comparable degree of recovery from dependence, and repair of the related damage.

6

In the community therapy model that we use, and strongly endorse, a common clinical program is utilized, with additional special services for special groups when indicated. The treatment plan is directed to bringing all patients into more effective interaction with the community as a whole. We believe the emphasis today should be on the similarities rather than the differences between those who have become over-involved with chemical comforts and those who have not. To accomplish this, we believe the staff should consist of a balance of professional and non-professional personnel, males and females, and non-addicts and recovered addicts, at all levels of responsibility. When to this is added a first-come, first-served admissions policy, with no special quotas according to age, sex, or social status, we believe the need for special programs for special groups can be kept to a minimum.

The Chemically Dependent Woman

Having indicated my reasons for endorsing general rather than special health programs, I must now recognize some of the reasons for giving consideration to the unique problems of the chemically dependent woman. Rather than undertake to deal with this issue in any depth, I shall quote from a recent newsletter article prepared by the United States National Institute on Alcohol Abuse and Alcoholism:

"stepped-up research on women's alcohol problems has illuminated some important differences in the alcohol problems of women versus men. Among them are:

Women, far more frequently than men, point to a specific life crisis as a precipitator of heavy drinking. The problems most frequently cited are those which threaten their role as wife and mother, including divorce, desertion, death of a family member, children leaving home, and obstetrical and gynecological problems.

Women alcoholics, far more than men, report a history of depression associated with their alcoholism. And because of the greater number of psychoactive drugs prescribed to women than men, more women alcoholics than men are cross-addicted.

7

Divorce rates for alcoholic women are much higher than for alcoholic men. Non-alcoholic wives are far more likely to remain with their alcoholic husbands, than are non-alcoholic husbands with their alcoholic wives.

Preliminary studies on the 'fetal alcohol syndrome' point to the probable danger of birth defects in the children of alcoholic mothers. Links between alcohol and child abuse and neglect have also been made."

Conclusions

1) Recent studies clearly indicate the need for specific clinical and educational programs to meet the problems and needs of chemically dependent women. Whenever possible, these programs should be an extension of existing community services, rather than separate operations.

2) Total intake habits should be considered as one important unit in a comprehensive health program.

3) The middle third of this century has permitted us to appreciate the many complex components of the health problems associated with intake habits; it must be hoped that the final third will be directed toward finding effective solutions.

Special Issues of Women in Therapy

by Susan Stephenson

What goes on when a woman goes to consult with a professional? What does she bring, and what does the doctor-counsellor-therapist put into the situation? Are goals and expectations convergent or divergent?

It is becoming more and more obvious to more and more people that the mental health theories we use in our work, on a day-to-day basis, contain a great deal of folk lore in the disguise of scientific knowledge. Many of our mental health theories reinforce cultural assumptions about women—that woman's prime, if not only role, is to be wife and mother; that woman's place is to nurture man; that women, in order to be considered mentally healthy, should be submissive, dependent, compliant, sensitive, emotional, unassertive. Healthy women are expected to be content with, or actually seek out, a life of self-sacrifice, in which the needs of others are seen as more important than their own.

In addition to this biased and one dimensional view of women, we have to contend with the fact that very little has been written about women's psychology, women's life crises. This omission leaves fertile ground for biases and imagination.

Dr. Stephenson is an associate professor in child psychiatry, Department of Psychiatry, University of British Columbia, Vancouver, and co-ordinator of the Canadian Psychiatric Association task force on women's issues.

For instance, the section on the American Identity in Erikson's *Childhood and Society* contains 17 pages on the identity development of the adolescent boy, but only one paragraph about the development of the adolescent girl.

Many theories are vague and overinclusive, so that practically anyone could be diagnosed as sick. This is related too, to the fact that the norms we have are based largely on longitudinal studies of white, middle-class males.

Some of our ideas about "normality", health, and sickness, may fit readily with some of the assumptions women patients or clients bring with them: women should never get angry; women's place is at home; every woman needs a man; aggressive women are nasty, etc. As professionals, we are more qualified and more able to question our assumptions, values, biases, than are many of the women who seek our help.

Now I am going to try to point out to you some areas that need special awareness, special sensitivity on your part—maybe a re-examination of your own values.

Slide 1. In her initial interview with a professional, the woman usually feels intimidated. Because of her socialization she is likely to be submissive, deferential, compliant, and uncritically accepting of advice, suggestions, prescriptions, etc. given to her by the professional. We have to recognize her feeling of inequality, and guard against measures that tend to keep her in a one-down position rather than trying to develop a collaborative approach in which she takes appropriate responsibility for trying to deal with the problems of life.

Slide 2. The professional, in that first interview, often brings a training that has emphasized classification and diagnosis which will then lead to a treatment plan. Emotional problems cannot be approached in the same way as physical diseases. We are looking at a continuum, and at a multidimensional problem. However, our training, particularly medical training, has taught us to categorize, to put into boxes. For women, particularly, these don't fit or are used inappropriately.

To look at it in another way, we will go through a process designed to produce a diagnosis. *(Slide 3).* In addition to the problems I've already mentioned about deficiencies in mental health theories, I think we can often recognize a kind of informal diagnosis *(Slide 4)* which goes along with the formal diagnosis and can even, at times, replace it or assume major importance, in terms of how it affects the formal diagnostic process. These informal labels are often used in a pejorative and blaming sense, and obscure the fact there are problems with other family members, or with systems outside the family. For instance, in my experience, a single mother is almost inevitably assumed by almost everybody to have caused her children's problems. Many people, too, still fall into the trap of blaming the alcoholic's wife for his drinking problems. Many a husband is felt to be a nice guy suffering from the castrating, bitchy, unfeminine behavior of his nagging wife. We have to be aware of the seductive power of these informal labels, which reflect bias, prejudice and myth, and yet very readily creep in to cloud our objectivity and muddy the assessment process.

During initial interviews, goals may be set. Often this is not done explicitly and via discussion. The professional may have ideas about the woman's future adjustment *(Slide 5)* that are completely different from those of the woman herself. All too often, the therapist's goals reflect, as shown in the Broverman studies, the traditional feminine stereotype. Again, all too often, the woman herself, shares the view *(Slide 6)* that women should, in order to be mentally healthy, be feminine, nurturant, submissive, compliant and sensitive, and should not be assertive, competitive, outspoken, self-involved, angry etc.

Slide 7. We have to get beyond these stereotypes, for ourselves, and for the women who come to see us. Is our goal to make the woman *adjust?* To tell her she should be happy with her attractive body and her charming manner, or with her beautiful home, marvellous husband, and gorgeous children? Do we instruct her to become more proficient at using "feminine wiles" to get her way with her husband, without actually confronting him? Do we, as reported about one psychiatrist, tell her she should aim to look like Zsa Zsa Gabor?

Or, do we help her to focus on her own needs without feeling terribly guilty about wanting some time for herself and an identity of her own? Do we think about her personal growth, and help her to develop a life plan that is realistic and directed to her own needs as well as those of her family?

Do we recognize that conflict and pain are a necessary part of change, growth, maturing? Or, are we quick to prescribe tranquillizers with the feeling that she needs help to cope with her situation?

Hurdles

During therapy, it is vital to be constantly aware of the fact that society presents an obstacle course for women. We MUST not let ourselves be seduced by theories that present only an intrapsychic and individual basis for problems. There are many realistic outside pressures, expectations, obstacles, and in-equalities for women. Sometimes our job may be gradually to help a woman become aware of these obstacles and feelings which are universal to all women, and certainly not neurotic, but a consequence of belonging to a subordinate group. Feelings of helplessness, powerlessness, guilt, suppressed anger. It could be our job to work with a woman so she stops viewing herself as neurotic, and sees her difficulties as stemming from realistic environmental hurdles, not from herself.

Some of the hurdles:

Slide 8. Unequal pay. Women, on average, earn 54%-60% as much as men.

Slide 9. Unequal opportunity. Improving but still very much there.

Slide 10. Socialization. Brainwashed from an early age, women find it very difficult to feel comfortable about being assertive, angry, etc.

Slide 11. Woman's place. Everyone, including almost all women, retains traditional assumptions about this. Many career women do two jobs.

Slide 12. Legislation. Property. Problems such as wife-battering.

Slide 13. Stereotype. Job situations—women's work.

Slide 14. Medicalization of social problems, certainly doesn't apply just to women, has been discussed by writers such as Illich and Szasz. For women, problems of living, and problems related to the obstacles in their lives, are confused with psychiatric disorder.

Slide 15. The professional who is sensitive to this dimension helps the woman to jump over the hurdle.

Slide 16. The insensitive sexist dismisses her problem as an individual neurotic problem. He pushes her back.

We have, however, to avoid throwing the baby out with the bath-water and insisting that, for instance, consciousness raising, or assertiveness training, are all that are needed by any woman. Some women are locked into vicious self-fulfilling prophecies about themselves and the world, and they need skilled counselling.

Dilemmas

Some of the dilemmas that can arise in counselling, to which women are particularly vulnerable, are:

Slide 17. Dilemma I. Here a person who has, or feels she has a disease, has abdicated responsibility. Women, socialized to be dependent, unassertive, compliant, may be more likely to agree with a diagnosis, less likely to challenge an authority figure, and seem to fall into the helpless and powerless position of feeling taken over by a disease process.

Slide 18. Dilemma II. Women are taught to be responsible for others, to be helpful, nurturant, supportive, kind. We are more likely to feel guilty about our husbands, children. We blame ourselves frequently and others blame us often. Often a "blame the victim" process happens, so that a mother gets blamed for her husband's incestuous relationship with their daughter, or the wife of an alcoholic for his alcoholism. We know people get stuck in a mental rut when they blame themselves. So it is important to be very sensitive to women's unique capacity to blame themselves for almost anything, and to work on self-blame as an issue that must be transcended.

Slide 19. Dilemma III. Another way of abdicating responsibility and avoiding the painful process of growing, is to blame all one's problems on a parent figure. This is, of course, a major focus of

13

dynamic theories. Women have worked on their Oedipal conflicts for years without getting in touch with their present day lives! For the therapist, decisions must be made around how much early childhood needs to be explored to liberate the person from the parental admonitions that they carry in their head; how much to focus on day to day realities.

Slide 20. Dilemma IV. Women need help and encouragement to see many of their problems in terms of societal obstacles. Beyond this, however, there may be some difficulties related to their own, individual, painful life experiences. The therapist has to work with the woman to keep an appropriate balance.

Slide 21. Dilemma V. This is, perhaps, a more recent dilemma for therapists.

We have to beware of unidimensional formulations of women's problems that arise from work on sex roles and motivation. To tell a woman, or agree with her, that her only problem is "fear of success" can be as limiting as telling her she suffers from penis envy.

I now want to comment on some problems that can arise in a therapeutic relationship, to which women seem particularly prone.

Slide 22. Dependency. Unfortunately, therapy may serve only to repeat a woman's experiences in a middle-class marriage. She becomes dependent on a male authority figure who may, himself, find this very gratifying, fulfilling his need to be needed. This dependency is paralyzing and must be avoided in order to promote the woman's growth and ability to think for herself. The involvement of the family, or other support system, is crucial, thus avoiding the formation of an intense, binding, one-to-one relationship, which isolates the woman even further from other relationships.

Slide 23. Hostile Dependency. Again this is very common in man/ woman, husband/wife, and therapist/patient relationships. The woman can't express her anger overtly, so she employs needling, digs, subtle putdowns. She sabotages, says "yes, but ...", gets at you by quoting another professional, or something she's read in the paper. She can't get mad, but she can't leave the relationship because she's afraid she can't manage on her own. She needs to have her anger recognized and validated, along with her fears, before she can grow towards independence and autonomy.

Slide 24. Regression. Under stress, people regress and become more childish. This is, however, promoted in women as a desirable trait. Recently, I was at a wedding where the bride was described as an "ideal combination of childlike naiveté and sophistication." Analytically-oriented therapists postulate that many women fail to resolve the Oedipal conflict and are thus prone to forming childlike, dependent relationships with men. My own feeling is that this is more an expression, in this culture, of the little girl's perception of father as a very powerful figure compared to mother, who seems powerless. In any event, programmed to feel helpless and childlike, women need special attention to their need to develop autonomy and independence, and an identity of their own, beyond their family and beyond the therapist as a substitute parental figure.

Slide 25. Unquestioning Obedience. The woman obeys the powerful authority figure, the professional. He says: "You are neurotic". She agrees. He says: "You need these pills". She does. He says: "You should look more feminine". She tries. She asks for aid with decisions about the most seemingly trivial things. The therapist is put on a pedestal. He/she must see the unhelpful nature of this interaction, or rather lack of interaction, with an apparently "model patient" who faithfully obeys all suggestions and carries them out to the letter. If the therapist continues to give suggestions etc., the woman will never take responsibility for herself. Her deeper underlying feelings will stay hidden, and the encounter will remain a very superficial one or a stalemate.

Slide 26. Inarticulate. Often, a woman will say very little. She is scared, unassertive, guilty, does not really know what she wants. Lacking much in the way of an identity of her own, tending, as women do, to rely on affirmation from the males in their lives, she is terribly afraid of being judged by the therapist authority figure. Thus, she tries to say what she thinks the therapist thinks she should say, tries to wear what she thinks she should wear, and tries to look and act the way she thinks he thinks she should.

15

She is overwhelmed by the "shoulds" and if she's aware of any anger, keeps it tightly inside. A therapist needs to be gentle, perceptive, and empathic, in order to work with this woman, so she can begin to state HER feelings, begin to define HER identity, feel free to express HER feelings, start to plan her life in terms of HER needs as a person. Therapists often get annoyed or frustrated by the inarticulate woman and may think she is "really sick" or dismiss her as "unmotivated" for therapy. This latter judgement is, one feels, more often applied to lower class, or minority group women, to whom ethnic as well as female stereotypes may be applied.

Slide 27. Mutual Seduction. This is fairly common, BUT not talked about. The expression varies from flirting to sexual intercourse, in a few cases. Flirting keeps the relationship at a superficial or game-playing level, which is much more comfortable for the woman than dealing with painful, deeper feelings. After all, flirting is something she is probably used to. The woman who engages in mutual flirtation with the therapist will feel good that she is attractive to such a powerful person. At another level, however, she may be aware of feelings of betrayal and worthlessness, thinking "here is yet another person, supposedly an expert, who isn't really interested in me as a person, but just as a body".

Although both woman and therapist may enjoy a sexualized relationship, it is really another variety of stalemate, and can be very destructive to the woman. Women are very vulnerable to sexual exploitation in such relationships. They may, at first, think sex has been helpful, but inevitably, according to Marmor, they end up feeling betrayed, humiliated, and embarrassed, and frequently blame themselves.

We, as therapists, have a great responsibility to avoid using our clients/patients in any kind of sexual sense, to compensate, perhaps, for a lack in our own lives. A woman treated by society as a sex object, desperately needs a therapist who will not deal with her on this level, but will see through any attempt on her part to use sexuality as an avoidance technique, and gently remind her that the therapist's role is to collaborate with her in understanding herself as a person, and her needs, fears, conflicts, and goals.

16

Slide 28. Set Up Rejection. Because of her feelings of worthlessness, or because of fears of parent and authority figures in her life, the woman may set up rejection situations by being provocative, testing, making scenes. It has been customary for the therapist to react to these situations by calling the woman an hysteric, a label that seems to have pejorative tones, and seems to call for an authoritarian and directive attitude on the part of the therapist. A controlling and impersonal approach will possibly alienate her further, so a vicious circle gets set up.

Some general principles

- The social context must always be kept in mind;
- It must be remembered it is a collaborative relationship;
- Awareness of one's own values and biases is essential;
- One must have a critical attitude towards theoretical background, process of diagnosis.

1

2

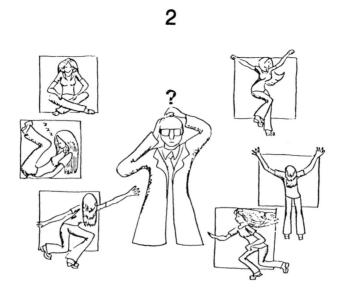

3

Diagnosis

HYSTERICAL? PERSONALITY?

DEPRESSIVE?

NEUROTIC?

MANIC DEPRESSIVE?

OBSESSIVE?

COMPULSIVE?

CHRONIC ALCOHOLISM?

4

Informal Diagnosis

OVERPROTECTIVE?

MARTYR?

TYPICAL
ALCOHOLIC'S WIFE?

SEDUCTIVE?

SINGLE MOTHER?

DEPENDENT?

Bitchy?
Castrating?
Nag?
Unfeminine?

19

7

Goals ?

ADJUST ?

COPE ?

GROWTH ?

CONFLICT ?

8

Hurdles-1

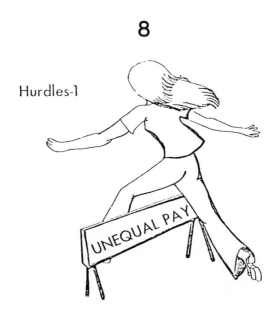

9

2

10

3

11

12

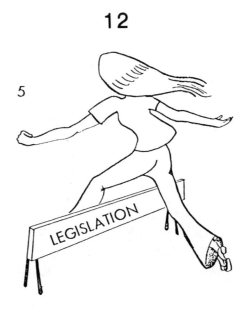

13

6

STEREOTYPING

14

7

MEDICALIZATION OF SOCIAL PROBLEMS

15

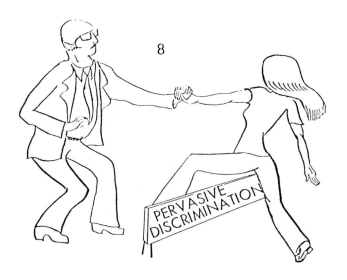

8

16

9

17

DILEMMA 1

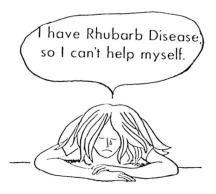

18

DILEMMA 2

19

DILEMMA 3

20

DILEMMA 4

21

DILEMMA 5

22

DEPENDENCY

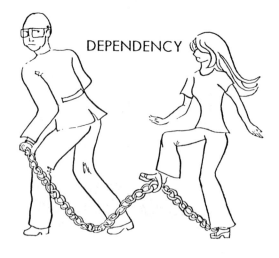

23

HOSTILE 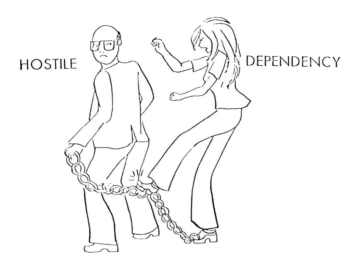 DEPENDENCY

24

REGRESSION

25

MUTUAL SEDUCTION

26

SETS
UP

REJECTION

27

UNQUESTIONING OBEDIENCE

28

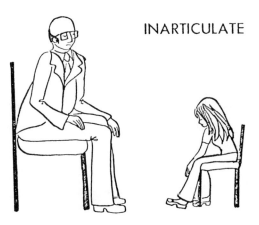

INARTICULATE

Getting in Touch With The Chemically Dependent Woman

by Lavada Pinder

There is no lack of opportunity for deliverers of social and health care services to be in touch with chemically dependent women. Simply in terms of numbers, there is increasing evidence that more women are drinking, and more women are becoming alcoholic. Recent estimates in Ontario indicate that nearly a quarter of a million citizens are alcoholic. Missing statistical links prevent accurate estimates of how many might be women. There are, however, some available figures which are useful in coming to terms with the dimensions of the problem. For example, both The Donwood Institute and the Addiction Research Foundation treatment program in Ottawa-Carleton, report ratios of three men to every woman. The World General Service Committee of Alcoholics Anonymous, in their 1974 survey, reported that one-third of new entries were women. Early estimates of their 1976 survey indicate that closer to one half of newcomers are women. There is the added knowledge that many of these women will be cross-dependent and many others dependent on psychotropics alone, given the female consumption rate of mood-changing drugs.

The point of emphasizing the growing number of women

Ms Pinder is director of the Ottawa-Carleton program of the Addiction Research Foundation, Ottawa.

33

with alcohol and drug problems, is to heighten the consciousness of all social and health care workers that, knowingly and
unknowingly, they are encountering chemically dependent
women in their day-to-day practice. The challenge is to make all
of these encounters ones which count in the enormous task of
reaching and helping these women.

Obstacles

Despite the variety of opportunities for getting in touch with
chemically dependent women, there are obstacles which
prevent open, meaningful encounters. The phenomenon of
denial is legendary in the field of alcoholism. Where women are
concerned, the problems are compounded, for not only do
women deny, but social and health care workers can be
collaborators. The process of covering up is mutual and both
parties in the transaction—patient-doctor, client-counsellor,
deliverer-consumer—faithfully reflect societal attitudes and
practices.

Most social and health care workers have been trained
subtly, and not so subtly, to believe that treating alcoholics is
unrewarding and that women do not have the problem. By
subtle, I mean the fact alcohol and drug studies are either
completely omitted, or given only slight recognition, in
professional curricula. By unsubtle, I mean that some clinicians
who serve as models for students, verge on the punitive in their
attitudes to alcoholics.

There is also the impact of their own alcohol consumption
on the perceptions of social and health care workers. If they
drink a lot, there can be a tendency to underestimate abuse in
others. If they are abstinent, or drink very little, there can be the
tendency to overestimate others' drinking. Here it is interesting
to note that drug and alcohol problems among physicians are
significantly higher than in the general population.

Most important, is the double standard of mental health
based on assumptions which have permeated the health and
social care delivery system to women, and influenced countless
practitioners.

On the other hand, the consumer of service will make every

effort to cover up her problem of alcoholism, preferring to present what she believes to be more acceptable symptoms. The reasons for this are two-fold. She is aware of the disapproval with which society views alcoholic women. At the same time, she has become dependent on alcohol and/or drugs to ease her particular pain of living. Certainly, a major obstacle to any alcoholic opening up about the problem is the knowledge that the treatment of this treatable illness will be giving up alcohol, a prospect every alcoholic fears.

Overcoming these obstacles requires health and social care workers to get in touch not only with issues of drug and alcohol dependency, but also women's issues. Helpers must begin to wrestle with their attitudes toward women's role, status, and aspirations, recognizing their meaning on an emotional and practical level. Helpers must take time to become informed about chemical dependency and the intervention strategies their particular discipline can bring into play. To tackle one of these issues without the other is to be partially equipped. By confronting and integrating both, social and health care workers have a good chance of getting "in touch", truly able to engage women with alcohol and drug problems in the pursuit of their own health.

In view of the enormity of the problem, it may seem to be a very modest approach to narrow the issue to deliverer-consumer transactions. Because of this, I want to be clear that this transaction must be seen within the social context in which it takes place. It must be recognized that these transactions take place within systems and structures frequently designed to maintain existing attitudes and practices. For example, women are most affected by these issues, have the greatest stake in it, and therefore have the greatest commitment to change. However, there is an absence of women in positions where policies are made which affect delivery of service. Another example is the fact that while women make up something like 90% of the health care workers, only 8% of physicians are women, and health delivery systems tend to be headed by medical doctors. It is true that work is being done to change these systems and alter these statistics. However, it is an unjoyful message that systems do not change rapidly and, in the meantime, practitioners must begin.

Opportunities

There are natural opportunities within service deliveries to begin recognizing and treating women with chemical dependency problems. There are strategies which emerge simply by exploring the roles that we, as social and health care workers, play out in day-to-day practice.

There are three opportunities which can be singled out and which fall within the responsibilities of most social and health care workers. Education, assessment, and crisis intervention represent functions which can take on meaning in the prevention and intervention aspects of working with women with chemical dependency.

Education is a vital way to reach many women. There is the education of self and the education of consumers of service. They go hand in hand. Education of consumers can range from the low-keyed approach of distributing pamphlets and displaying posters, to orientation of all consumers to facts related to drugs and alcohol. Regardless of approach, it is the steady, long-term inclusion of education materials and instruction which has impact and contributes to demystifying the subject.

If assessment is considered ongoing, then not only will queries related to drug and alcohol involvement and their linkage to presenting social and psychological problems figure prominently at intake, but practitioners will continuously be mindful that women may be finding chemical solutions to social problems. Once again, it is the constant attention to these issues which pays off. When it can be noted that in a recent survey of social and health care workers in Ottawa-Carleton, 44% of those interviewed did not ask questions about drug and alcohol use, then it is not inappropriate to make this suggestion.

Crisis is considered by many in the addictions field to present excellent potential for intervention. Women will respond to help when a crisis makes alcohol an unattractive solution. It is at these times that social and health care workers can be at the ready, knowledgeable about resources, aware of alternatives, sensitive to a woman's potential to change.

To you who already have added these tasks to your work, I say ... build. To those of you who do not, I say ... begin.

Women and Psychotropic Drug Use

by Ruth Cooperstock

A major difference between the clients Lavada (Pinder) was talking about and those I will be talking about, is that virtually everybody using psychotropic drugs or medications has received them through a representative of our health care system. Consequently, I am going to talk to you about our health care system and the people receiving drugs from it.

We know that about 95% of those who use legal psychotropic drugs, like tranquillizers, receive them from a prescription written in their own name.

What drugs are we talking about, when we say psychotropic drugs? Primarily, we are talking about the benzodiazepines that Dr. (R. Gordon) Bell already mentioned. In common parlance, these are most of the drugs called minor tranquillizers: Valium®, Librium®, Vivol®, etc. You all know them. We're talking about the sedative-hypnotic drugs, the barbiturates, and the non-barbiturates. To a much lesser extent, we're talking about stimulant drugs which, as you know, have almost disappeared from Canada because of a law change a couple of years back; anti-depressants which are not a problematic drug except among the elderly; and the major tranquillizers, the anti-psychotic

Ms Cooperstock is a scientist in social studies at the Addiction Research Foundation, Toronto.

39

agents which are problematic in terms of some side effects, but are prescribed to a much lesser extent than minor tranquillizers.

Close to half of all psychotropic drugs prescribed today are minor tranquillizers and this has risen very rapidly in the last few years. Additionally, and it is important to be aware of this, the benzodiazepines cut across the usual classification systems and are found among the minor tranquillizers, hypnotics, anti-convulsants, and anti-cholinergics. For example, one of the most commonly prescribed sleeping medications today is a drug called Dalmane®. It is a benzodiazepine which is chemically similar, though not identical, to other benzodiazepines, but is prescribed in doses high enough to induce sleep instead of just mild sedation.

Having told you what drugs I'm talking about, and concentrating on the minor tranquillizers, especially the ben-zodiazepines, we can ask: who prescribes these drugs, where do people get them?

Virtually all studies indicate that most of these drugs are prescribed by general practitioners. This is essentially because they are general drugs, prescribed in response to vague, poorly-defined symptoms of the sort people bring to their family doctors. Now, we might ask: who receives these drugs? Which groups within our society, by which I mean Western indus-trialized society, are at highest risk of receiving these drugs? (Studies in many industrialized countries have shown similar distribution patterns of these drugs). The first and most obvious high risk population, as you are aware, I'm sure, is women. Additionally, the elderly, the chronically ill, and institutionalized are at high risk for receipt of psychotropic drugs.

Let us concentrate first, on how much drug people receive. In a study conducted here in Toronto a number of years ago, we found, on average, the adult population received just under one prescription per year per person for a psychotropic drug. Since most prescriptions are written for a 30-day supply, that can translate to 30 days worth per adult per year. A more recent study in Winnipeg, using exactly the same methods, came up with a figure slightly higher than this. When you look at the distribution of these drugs to males and females, you find females receiving almost two-and-a-half times the number of psychotropic drugs that males do. The average female in the Winnipeg study, receives about 45 days' supply per year; the average male about 15 days' supply. It is difficult to interpret these figures because we don't know if a few people received steady prescriptions over the year, or if many people received one or two. However, studies indicate that if you ask people what drugs they have taken in the last two weeks, about 20% of the women will reply they have used a psychotropic drug, mostly tranquillizers. That's one out of every five adult females.

Now we can ask, as some people do, is this a problem? Some say these are reasonably safe drugs, therefore what is the problem? I will go very quickly through what I, and many others, perceive to be the problem, on the assumption that most of us wouldn't be here today unless we were concerned with issues related to consumption of these substances. I will mention a few of them without going into any great detail.

The first and most obvious hazard in benzodiazepine use is that most people taken to hospitals having overdosed themselves with drugs have done so with Valium,® and in combination with alcohol or some other drug. These overdosed patients, appearing at hospitals, are primarily young females.

The second hazard is the risk of fetal damage. There are increasing numbers of studies examining fetal damage in relation to the use of benzodiazepines. There is little certainty at this moment, although these drugs have been on the market for 15 years. Longitudinal studies examining fetal damage are just being initiated. There have been two major studies from the United States indicating birth defects as a result of benzodiazepine use. It may be interesting for you to hear what all United States advertisements for benzodiazepines now say about their use during pregnancy. They must say:
A major difference between the clients Lavada (Pinder) was talking about and those I will be talking about, is that virtually everybody using psychotropic drugs or medications has received them through a representative of our health care system. Consequently, I am going to talk to you about our health care system and the people receiving drugs from it.

We know that about 95% of those who use legal psychotropic drugs, like tranquillizers, receive them from a prescription written in their own name.

What drugs are we talking about, when we say psychotropic drugs? Primarily, we are talking about the benzodiazepines that Dr. (R. Gordon) Bell already mentioned. In common parlance, these are most of the drugs called minor tranquillizers: Valium®, Librium®, Vivol®, etc. You all know them. We're talking about the sedative-hypnotic drugs, the barbiturates, and the non-barbiturates. To a much lesser extent, we're talking about stimulant drugs which, as you know, have almost disappeared from Canada because of a law change a couple of years back; anti-depressants which are not a problematic drug except among the elderly; and the major tranquillizers, the anti-psychotic agents which are problematic in terms of some side effects, but are prescribed to a much lesser extent than minor tranquillizers.

Close to half of all psychotropic drugs prescribed today are minor tranquillizers and this has risen very rapidly in the last few years. Additionally, and it is important to be aware of this, the benzodiazepines cut across the usual classification systems and are found among the minor tranquillizers, hypnotics, anti-convulsants, and anti-cholinergics. For example, one of the most commonly prescribed sleeping medications today is a drug called Dalmane®. It is a benzodiazepine which is chemically similar, though not identical, to other benzodiazepines, but is prescribed in doses high enough to induce sleep instead of just mild sedation.

"An increased risk of congenital malformation associated with the use of minor tranquillizers, e.g., diazepam, during the first trimester of pregnancy has been suggested in several studies. Because use of these drugs is rarely a matter of urgency, their use during this period should almost always be avoided. The possibility that women of child-bearing potential may be pregnant at the time of institution of the therapy should be considered. Patients should be advised that if they become pregnant during therapy, or intend to become pregnant, they should communicate with their physicians about the desirability of discontinuing the drug."

I am sorry to say, our Canadian advertisements are not yet required to carry such warnings.

Then there is the problem that many of us are concerned about. That is the failure of physicians to examine for physical or somatic disorders and the prescribing of these drugs for so-called neurotic problems, sometimes masking somatic illnesses.

An additional series of problems, which those of you who work in the addictions field are aware of, are problems of cross-addiction to alcohol, of dependence, of impaired motor skills, of other kinds of physical deficits, and of a variety of secondary side effects.

There are also what we can call the social hazards which, unfortunately, have been explored much less adequately than the physical hazards. We might talk about social toxicity in relation to these drugs. What does tranquillization of one family member do to family life? What does it do to the interaction of mothers and young children? What does it do to sex life? We know what barbiturates do. What does chronic use of tranquillizers do to the way people view themselves, to their self-images? Does it permit individuals to mask their problems or difficulties? Does it permit the physician comfortably to overlook asking about difficulties in his patient's life situation? Because of this evasion, does it assure a continuance of the individual within the health care system and the continued dependence on the physician that Dr. (Susan) Stephenson talked about, precisely because no one is looking at the causes of problems? If this does occur, what does it do to the cost of our health care system which everyone is so concerned about these days? These are some of the problems we call social toxicity.

The next question we might ask is: is there a difference in the way physicians prescribe to patients of different statuses or fulfilling different roles?

To answer this, I would like to describe a study conducted recently at the University of Western Ontario in their Family Practice Clinic. This clinic is part of a teaching hospital, and they carried out what might be called a critical test. They included for study, men and women who presented with exactly the same symptoms: problems of emotional disturbance, such as crying, depression, nervousness, etc. They examined the treatments offered to these patients over the course of the next year and found that on the first visit in particular, the males were more likely to be sent for laboratory tests, or to be given some physical therapy. The males and females were equally likely to be sent for counselling, or referral to social agencies. The only major difference between the sexes in their therapeutic regime was that the females received significantly more minor tranquillizer prescriptions than the males and, over time, the difference increased, so that six months later there was a larger difference than there was at the first visit. We can now say with confidence that doctors *do* prescribe more of these drugs to females even when the patients present with the same symptoms.

There are many reasons for this behavior. Let me give you a very quick illustration of one of the reasons from a brochure advertising Valium®. It makes the claim that Valium® is the only drug that is truly effective for three major conditions: first, for psychotherapeutic uses, such as diminishing anxiety, tension; second, as a muscle relaxant; and third, as an anti-convulsant. The individual depicted as needing it for psychotherapeutic reasons is a woman of child-bearing years, while it's a male who needs a muscle relaxant, and a male who needs an anti-convulsant. This is what many of you have observed over the years in drug advertising. We had hoped that, gradually, this would diminish. Unfortunately, it hasn't yet disappeared, this kind of advertising which stereotypes, which reinforces, and which we're not aware of when it occurs unless we're really looking for it.

Epidemiologists and sociologists who have studied health statistics over time are very aware of the old saw that "women get sick but men die." That is, males die at a younger age than females, but females report more illnesses; females go to doctors somewhat more than males, although it's mostly in certain age groups. This poses a bit of a dilemma. What does it mean?

I think it's important that we look at some of the models used to account for these differences in the illness experiences of men and women. There are three basic models that have been used as explanations. The first simply states that women report more illnesses than men because it's culturally more

44

acceptable for them to be ill, to be aware of their physical reactions, and to report themselves as ill. The common notion is that the ethic of positive health is masculine. It starts with little boys who are told they can't cry, they shouldn't admit to feeling ill. The second model says that the sick role is relatively compatible with women's other role responsibilities and incompatible with those of men. Men have to go to work, to keep rigid time schedules; women have more "leisure." Additionally, women are the monitors of health of their families, so their role allows them to be more in touch with sickness and health. The third model says that women's assigned social roles are so stressful today that they have more illness than men.

The first two models are really talking about illness behaviors as distinct from clinical illnesses. That is, they are reports of visits to doctors, reports of days ill, reports of feelings or symptoms. Only the last model says women are actually sicker than men. Illness behavior such as going to doctors, reporting symptoms or days home, has the potential to result in a prescription for a tranquillizer.

We now have to ask: what are the differences in illness behaviors between those who occupy different social roles? That might give us a clue as to whether women are, in fact, sicker or whether we are talking about only illness behaviors as distinct from actual illness. We really want to know the relationship between what individuals report of their illnesses and what drugs they are prescribed, particularly psychotropic drugs. How well do they match? We know, for example, that the elderly suffer much more chronic illness, that they also use medical services much more than younger adults, that they receive many more prescriptions—about two and a half times the proportion of prescriptions that younger people do. But they don't receive a very much higher proportion of tranquillizing drugs than do people in their middle years, although they unfortunately receive many more barbiturates and other sedative-hypnotic drugs. In this example, we find a group who are more frequently ill than others, whose illness behavior reflects this, and for whom psychotropic drug use is generally high. Let us examine some other roles quickly and see what we do know about the illness behavior of people fulfilling these roles.

Studies indicate that women with young children in their homes report they're sick less often, and report fewer symptoms and fewer days of illness, than women of the same age who don't have young children at home. We know, too, that women who live on the upper floors of apartment buildings report more illness, go to doctors more often, and use other health services more than women who live on lower floors, or than women who live in private homes.

What are these data saying? They're saying something, I think, about social isolation and the need for help. The Winnipeg study mentioned earlier asked about social activities as well as drug consumption. They found that women who belong to more organizations, who get out of their houses more, whether they are working or not, and who engage in sports and in varieties of voluntary organizations, report use of fewer psychotropic drugs and, attend doctors less often than less active women.

Related to social activity is work status. This is one of the most important variables to look at in relation to women today. Employed women use health services less and report fewer symptoms than the unemployed or women who work only in their homes. The people who use the most psychotropic drugs are those who report themselves to be working in their own homes, housewives, and unemployed.

A recent study of psychotropic drug use in women shows an interesting continuum in relation to employment. Of those not in the work force, 25% reported having used a psychotropic drug in the previous two weeks; among part time workers, the comparable figure was 19%; and among those working full time, 11%. It seems quite clear, examining variables such as employment status or social activity, that roles in society are important in understanding drug consumption.

The health care service generally provided views its function as helping individuals come to terms with their roles in society. If someone fulfilling one of those roles, e.g., a socially inactive person not employed outside her home, goes to her doctor and complains of tension, nerves, anxiety, low back pain, headache, stress, etc., is it adequate to get rid of these symptoms with tranquillizers?

Many individuals use tranquillizers to maintain themselves in certain roles. For example, I recently talked to a woman who has been on tranquillizers for 10 years. She has five teenaged children and had quit work in order to raise them. She said: "I use these drugs for one purpose and one purpose only—I use them to protect my family from my irritability."

What could be a better description of a female's nurturing role? But how does this affect her family, how does this affect her relationships, how angry is this woman underneath all these medications she's been on for 10 years?

I have attempted to point out to those of you working in the health care system that it is necessary to examine, and understand, and perhaps help, individuals alter the roles they play, as well as their individual psyches. In that way, you may be helping people to a richer, a fuller, a better life through examining their life situations, rather than only their feelings of tension and anxiety.

The Chemical Trap: A Patient's View

by Jean O'Brien

When I was asked to speak at this seminar, I accepted without hesitation, and just as quickly chose my topic—The Chemical Trap. Since I am a former Donwood patient, what I have to say will be a personal history of sorts, but over the last three years I have had the opportunity to be closely associated with many other patients—one year as a recovering patient in our Phase III; the next year as a volunteer, working in an evening group for cross-addicted patients; and the last year on the Donwood staff as a therapist in a special drug group. More and more I have come to know the reality of the chemical trap.

Dr. (R. Gordon) Bell, in his book *Escape from Addiction* describes the trap. He states: "A great variety of chemicals— such as alcohol—are capable of producing enjoyment even when poisonous quantities are used—therein lies the danger of the chemical trap."

We encounter the drugs by social custom, occupational routine, medical prescription, status seeking, and they all have the very important property—the ability to improve the way we feel. To quote Dr. Bell: "Continued use develops tolerance; our body adjusts to the impact of those chemicals, and even greater

---

Ms. O'Brien is a health counsellor at The Donwood Institute.

and/or more frequent doses are required to achieve the same pleasurable effect. When tolerance develops to the degree that distressing symptoms occur with abstinence, then tolerance has become dependence, and desire has become sick need. The chemical trap has sprung."

The terrifying, really insidious part of the chemical trap is that once you begin to use a drug regularly, be it the drug alcohol or another mood-changing chemical, you are impairing your ability to cope, to make decisions. In fact, you are impairing your ability to look realistically at, or deal with, the problems or situations that caused your distress. Your reason for wanting a chemical escape becomes foggy, you can no longer honestly identify your emotions. Caught in this circle, you lose your ability to understand, or even to recognize your own entrapment.

When the chemical being used has been prescribed by a doctor, another important component is added: you are consciously, or perhaps unconsciously, relieved of the responsibility of how you feel, you are being told "you need medication."

I can remember as if it were yesterday, the relief I felt when my psychiatrist, on my first visit to him, prescribed lithium carbonate. "It wasn't me," I told myself, "it was something inside, beyond my control, a chemical imbalance of sorts, that was going to be set right." Prior to this, I had asked my gynecologist to refer me to an endocrinologist, feeling sure there must be something wrong with my metabolism. He had found nothing.

You see, I had been searching for an answer for some time. Here I was, an intelligent, healthy young woman, the envy of many. I had everything I had been "programmed" to strive for and achieve. A university education, securely married to a very successful professional man, three happy, healthy, well-adjusted children. No problems there! On top of that, a beautiful big home, complete with swimming pool, near my parents and childhood home, membership in the so-called "best" clubs, and at least four holidays a year, skiing and travelling to conventions. Isn't that what every 35-year-old woman needs to make her happy? Of course it is. I was told this over and over, by my husband, my parents, the media, and some of my friends.

So, what's wrong? Why isn't entertaining, doing volunteer work, cleaning "House Beautiful," playing bridge, playing tennis, looking after three children, and being an asset to my husband, enough? My goodness, what more do you want? "Must be something wrong with me".

Why am I getting depressed for days on end, feeling tired and unloved, crying by myself? Then, a few days later, why am I going into a fury of activity, painting and papering, planning a party, getting a stack of 15 books from the library, completely convinced I'll read them all in a week. "Must be something wrong with me."

I get angry, but not for long. That's not pretty, or the way to please others. I get demanding of my husband's time, but not for long. After all, what's he working for but me and the children? I should be thankful he's so successful and works three or four nights a week. And the weekends? Well, of course he needs some relaxation, so what better way than golf with the boys? I'm not always the best company anyway. Starting to complain too much. "There must be something wrong with me." I take up golf, but I don't like it. "Must be something wrong with me."

Time goes by. Children in school all day, keep busy, but still unhappy. My husband tells me: "If you can't be happy with all this, there must be something wrong with you. I've got the name of one of the best psychiatrists in the city, you need to see him." I agree. Well, the psychiatrist agrees. My unhappiness and mood swings did seem inappropriate to him, but we could look after that, thus the lithium carbonate, and my relief. Now at last the problem had been solved. *I needed medication.* I would even have to go for blood tests while taking this. Who can control their own blood? So we'd found the answer. Or had we?

After one month, I found my mood swings had changed all right, but something was wrong. This drug had taken away my good old highs when I got things done, and left me only my lows. What's this? We can fix that without any trouble. Here's an anti-depressant, take three a day. A caution here: don't eat old cheese or red wine. Anything else is okay. But, now I must see the psychiatrist weekly. Two weeks pass and I'm not feeling too relieved by all this—a little too anxious really to benefit from therapy, the doctor feels, must be calmed down. So, try some Trilafon® three a day. They're awful! Now my hands are trembling all day. No problem, we'll switch to Valium,® absolutely no side effects, no trembling, three or four 10 mg tablets a day. Next, you guessed it, within a month my sleep pattern was shot. Well, what did I expect? I was uncovering some unpleasant childhood experiences every Tuesday at 2 p.m. So sleeping pills were prescribed—Mandrax,® one at bedtime, another if I woke before 2 a.m.

I came to look forward to my visits to the doctor. He was a kind man, concerned and interested in me, which was pretty heady medicine itself! My husband didn't have time to go to see him as was requested, but things were definitely improving for everyone around me. I was crying less, didn't have the periods of frenzied activity, didn't get angry, didn't complain too much. I'd become "a good little girl" again, to everyone's great relief.

At this point, I'll sketch my drinking history since it does show the influence of pre-disposing factors in alcoholism. First of all, I had a high tolerance for alcohol. I didn't start to drink until university, and then only on special occasions or in a pub with a gang when I'd have one or two beers. Even at parties when I drank quite a bit, I was never sick, never had a hangover. After marriage, my husband was still in university, so our budget was such that we could rarely afford liquor.

It's interesting to look back to see the social influence on my alcoholic intake. As we became more and more affluent, entertained more, travelled and went to conventions, my consumption kept increasing. From a weekend party pattern, to cocktails before dinner, to adding wine with dinner, and later a liqueur after dinner. On holidays, it would be champagne breakfasts plus cocktails, wine, and liqueurs. This was expected and accepted. This pattern became the norm.

It's also enlightening to look at my psychological climate prior to alcoholism. Unlike many patients I have come to know, I didn't use alcohol to help me feel at ease or converse in a social situation. But I did come to use it to relieve the tension I felt in my marriage, to escape looking at the reality of loneliness and boredom, and to gloss over the lack of communication and sharing between my husband and myself.

Six months before Donwood, I experienced my first blackout. It was frightening. But, when I mentioned it to my husband and the couple we were travelling with at the time, they had all experienced blackouts before, so I conveniently set that fear aside. I was aware I was drinking daily, conscious of making sure there was always liquor or wine in the house, and of always choosing a restaurant with a liquor licence. I was drinking too much. I was having more frequent blackouts but I wasn't an alcoholic, I told myself. I didn't drink in the morning. My idea of a female alcoholic was a sloppy woman who neglected herself, her children, and her home—a woman who was an embarrassment to her family and the talk of the neighborhood. I didn't fit the picture, so I set that fear aside. I was looking after everything—not as well as before, mind you, and I needed so many lists, and couldn't seem to concentrate, sleeping so much. But I still got up every morning with the children, played bridge weekly, went skiing, etc. I couldn't be an alcoholic.

Four months prior to my admission to Donwood, my depressions and blackouts became more severe. I increasingly had a feeling of despair and total hopelessness. I was still seeing the psychiatrist on a weekly basis and told him of my blackouts and alcoholic intake. His comment about the alcohol was: "Hell, I drink more than that myself." During the blackouts, I am told, I was screaming and angry one moment, and despondent and suicidal the next. Finally, my husband contacted the doctor and I entered hospital—the psychiatric ward. Here I was taken off lithium and the anti-depressants, but continued with Valium® during the day and very heavy medication at night.

My five weeks in hospital were strange. I enjoyed talking to everyone and helped the O.T. woman daily. I even went out shopping for Christmas decorations for the ward. We went to movies and concerts, cooked a few meals. I felt very guilty about being away from home and my children but kept telling myself this was to help me get better. The weekends I went home were disastrous. My husband would have the martinis waiting, I'd have my bottles of medication from the hospital, and the blackouts and despair would start all over again. While I was in hospital, they gave me an E.E.G. before and after my drinking 4 oz of vodka. They had wondered if I was allergic to alcohol. Nothing irregular showed up, but I had a nice afternoon nap.

After discharge from the hospital, I resumed my weekly visits to the doctor and all the old medication except the lithium. Things went downhill once again. After a very unhappy ski holiday over Christmas, I felt my trap. I didn't know what to do, I couldn't think of any solutions. So, when my husband handed me a piece of paper with a phone number and the name of Dr. D.W. Macdonald (executive director and clinical director of The Donwood) on it, and told me to phone if I felt like it, I did. I had two meetings with Dr. Macdonald at Donwood. I wasn't really sure I was an alcoholic and didn't question my pill intake at all. But what he said made sense to me. Six weeks after those disquieting but very reassuring and hopeful sessions, I entered Donwood.

When I came into Donwood, I was confused, fearful, and feeling very guilty about leaving my children for hospital again. I felt as if I'd let everyone down. When I left four weeks later, I had some hope and faith in myself, and my future, for the first time in many years.

I've often been asked what did Donwood do for me? What was the most important ingredient? That's hard to say. It's rather like trying to decide what's the most important leg on a three-legged stool. You need the total package—the education, the nutrition, the relaxation and exercise, the insight gained in group therapy, and the care and support of both staff and patients—all of these woven into your new drug-free life. It's a unique experience.

I remember one morning so vividly. It was about eight days after my admission and I woke up to daylight and realized I'd slept for three-and-a-half hours without the help of medication. I hadn't done this for nearly four years. I burst into tears feeling such relief and hope.

The learning experience of the videos and discussions was stimulating: lights kept popping in my head as the stages of my addiction started to fit together. In group therapy, I remember crying on the first day and no one walked out or said: "Oh, you're being too emotional." In another group, we talked about getting in touch with our feelings (they were all starting to come back and bombard me now that I was free from drugs). Some of the feelings were anger, fear, rage, and that was okay. It was a heady experience indeed to feel these emotions and talk about them without someone saying: "You shouldn't feel that way." When someone in the group said they thought I was a "fighter," I can remember saying: "I used to be." But, gradually, I noticed that feeling of confidence and self-worth seeping back. It was wonderful. The great feeling that comes with recovery is hard to explain, but I think it's being able to label yourself a survivor. You're coming to life again after a very painful period.

About three months after leaving Donwood, I went back to see my psychiatrist, to confront him about the medication he had prescribed for me, and to tell him of my Donwood experience, among other things. He was obviously very happy and amazed to see me so exuberant and healthy. After our long talk he said this: "You and Donwood have done what I failed to do for you in three and a half years."

That is the story of my chemical trap.

The Chemical Trap: A Physician's Perspective

by Janet L. Dowsling

"In all countries, doctors work increasingly with two groups of addicts, those for whom they prescribe drugs and those who suffer from the consequences." Illich

As a family physician working in general practice, and as Co-ordinator of Medical Services at The Donwood Institute, I am painfully aware of the validity of Illich's comment and of the perils of the chemical trap. I see the physician's responsibility as fourfold: awareness of the problem, prevention, recognition, and referral.

Certainly, it has been well established by numerous studies that there has been a remarkable increase in the use of psychotropic medication, especially the benzodiazepines, Valium® and Librium®. It is uncertain whether this increase is because of the generally turbulent social climate, which has disturbed "one's place in the sun," the widespread promotion of new drugs, or because of the prescribing practices of clinicians.

It has become popular to blame multi-national pharmaceutical firms for the increase in medically prescribed drug abuse. Creating a market demand for a product is the most important function of advertising and the drug companies do it well. A

Dr. Dowsling is co-ordinator of medical services at The Donwood Institute, Toronto.

busy physician is exposed to subtly seductive advertising and will quite often respond by writing a prescription when he sees his next anxious or depressed patient, thus acting as "the instrumental consumer," and, perhaps unwittingly, "the pusher".

In 1972, Blackwell reported in JAMA (Journal of the American Medical Association) on prescription figures for psychotropic drugs among the 200 most popular drugs in the United States. He derived these figures from a monthly prescription audit of a national sample of 400 drugstores across the country. It showed that 97% of all general practitioners and internists used Valium® and 87% used Librium®, which ranked 1 and 3 respectively in popularity. Anti-depressants accounted for only 11% of the prescriptions.

You will notice that the companies have very subtly begun, in the case of psychotropics, to shift their emphasis from disease to "states of mind" which, it is implied, are diseases requiring treatment. In this way, what were formerly considered to be normal and often healing states of mind, such as anxiety, loneliness, grief, and even the forgetfulness of old age, have become symptoms of mental disease requiring treatment.

For many years, drug industry profits have outranked those of all other manufacturing industries listed on the stock exchange. The markup is most remarkable. Forty dollars of diazepam once stamped into pills and packaged as Valium® sells for 140 times as much. To promote Valium®, Hoffmann-LaRoche spent two hundred million dollars in 10 years, and commissioned some 200 doctors per year to produce scientific articles about its properties.

The more time and money spent by a population in producing medicine as a commodity, the greater the belief that it has a supply of "health locked away," and herein lies the "chemical trap." So, yes, the drug companies are involved in promoting a harmful dependence on their products, but patient expectation also plays a significant part in seeking a chemical solution to every problem, and a physician is at fault by "prescription."

Why are *these* drugs prescribed so frequently? The interesting thing to note in this market survey of physician use of diazepam (Valium®) is that the most prevalent diagnosis is mental disorders. These were unidentified, but the labels used to describe these emotions are usually anxiety and/or depression.

Preconceptions

Most patients consult their physician because of vague "ill health" and these symptoms are the physicians' gates to the pathway of problem solving. How do physicians, predominantly male, perceive the symptoms of their male and female patients? Studies suggest that the physician relies heavily on past experience, prior knowledge, and preconceptions when solving problems. Attitudes to, and perceptions of, male and female patients also affect diagnosis and treatment, according to a study done by Scottish general practitioners reported by Cooperstock. Almost twice the proportion of females to males were perceived as commonly reporting some form of mental disorder. The miscellaneous category of vague, poorly defined symptoms is the item that dramatically differentiates these physicians' views of their male and female patients.

A study by Vincent in 1974 shows the primary diagnosis of male and female physicians admitted to a Psychiatric Centre between 1950 and 1974, which also supports a sex differential in diagnosis. The primary diagnosis shows a higher incidence of psychoneurosis and a lower incidence of drug addiction and alcoholism among female physicians, but combining primary and secondary diagnoses among the females removes this difference. This suggests a possibility of a greater tendency to label the alcohol and drug problems in female physicians as secondary to the psychoneuroses, whereas the alcoholism and drug addictions were considered to be the primary diagnosis in the male physician. Work pressures would probably be discussed as the cause of male addiction versus psychoneuroses causing female addiction.

This table (Cooperstock) emphasizes again the perception of the physician of the frequency with which patients raise the following problems. You will notice that most of these problems were predominantly seen as female symptoms and, of course,

TABLE I *Physicians' perceptions of frequency with which patients raised the following problems:*

	Sleeplessness		Financial Difficulties		General Feelings of Unhappiness		Marital Discord		Headache		Disobedience of Children		Loneliness		Fatigue		Inability to concentrate	
	Male %	Female %	Male %	Female %	Male %	Female %	Male %	Female %	Male %	Female %	Male %	Female %	Male %	Female %	Male %	Female %	Male %	Female %
Frequently	13	79	4	11	4	53	11	34	17	83	-	6	4	15	19	79	11	26
Sometimes	49	21	34	51	45	45	40	62	47	15	6	47	26	62	68	19	66	53
Seldom	38	-	51	28	43	2	40	4	32	-	51	41	47	17	9	2	23	21
Never	-	-	9	6	6	-	6	-	2	-	40	6	21	6	2	-	-	-
No Answer	-	-	2	4	2	-	2	-	2	2	2	-	2	-	2	-	-	-
	47	47	47	47	47	47	47	47	47	47	47	47	47	47	47	47	47	47
	100	100	100	100	100	100	99	100	100	100	99	100	100	100	100	100	100	100

60

these "stresses of life" are exactly what prompt a prescription of a psychotropic drug. Are these problems a physician's concern, and what does the patient expect from the doctor?

Patients expect their doctor to give them a prescription and a study reported in the Canadian Medical Association Journal (January 1976) proves they usually get one. Physician-patient office contact lasts on the average 14 minutes. Two-thirds of these contacts result in a prescription, of which one-third will be for psychotropic agents. This study also showed a significant reduction in the use of sedatives and tranquillizers in the patients who were in the nurse-practitioner group versus the physician group, emphasizing that the nurse-practitioner group stressed the management of psychosocial problems with a minimal use of medication as a reflection of their training. The physician, on the other hand, is primed by her education to "cure all ills" and to do something, hence a prescription.

As a physician, I feel we have a responsibility to be aware of the dangers of prescribing medication to help women cope with every day "stresses of life."

After careful examination, these precautions in prescribing must be considered every time you take your prescription pad in hand: is the patient on any other medication? Is there any evidence of drug dependency? Is the real symptom a depression that might better be dealt with by using an anti-depressant? Is there any sign that there is some organic disease that might be causing increasing anxiety, for example, hyperthyroidism? Is there any indication of any psychiatric illness? For example, schizophrenia might present as an anxiety state with physical changes. And most importantly, have you asked your patient how much she is drinking, because anxiety and/or depression may be either a result of intoxication or withdrawal? Prescriptions should be short term, not repeated for infinity, and careful instructions should be given re usage. The dangers of combining psychotropic medications with alcohol should be emphasized.

Psychic Pain

Unfortunately, the psychic pain of the alcoholic is most often expressed in the doctor's office as anxiety and/or depression, to

61

which the doctor may respond by writing a prescription which only compounds the problem. This certainly shows in our figures at Donwood, with 27% of the women and 15% of the men cross-addicted on admission. Tranquillizers tend to mask the symptoms of alcoholism, allowing the condition to go untreated for long periods of time. As in all diseases, the earlier alcoholism can be diagnosed, faced by the patient, and initially treated, the easier it is to care for the illness.

The learned response of using a chemical for psychic pain is what renders the alcoholic patient open and vulnerable to drug substitution. In addition, the phenomenon of cross-tolerance makes it possible for the patient to consume these drugs in harmful quantities almost immediately on first experience. The reverse situation is also becoming a frequent occurrence. People addicted to drugs, particularly women dependent on tranquillizers, often secondarily become addicted to alcohol. The affect of minor tranquillizers is so similar to that of alcohol that their use by recovered alcoholics may precipitate a return to active drinking.

How can the chemical trap of prescribing psychotropic medication for your alcoholic patient be avoided? First of all, be highly suspicious: alcoholism should be the third most common diagnosis made. In addition to obtaining their usual complete history, the physician should obtain a drinking history from all patients. The drinking history should be designed to indicate the importance of alcohol to the patient and should explore areas of functional impairment caused by alcohol use.

This is a typical drinking history:

(1) type and frequency of beverage alcohol consumed;

(2) relationship of drinking to meal;

(3) whether tolerance to the drug is developing;

(4) whether there is a concomitant drug ingestion (tranquillizers, over-the-counter medications);

(5) evidence of emotional lability, increasing anxiety and depression, deteriorating interpersonal relationships, and substandard job performance. These can all be useful clues in determining whether alcohol abuse exists.

62

Knowledge of the pathophysiology of alcohol will allow the physician to relate alcohol abuse to abnormal physical findings. Although myriad signs can exist, the frequent physical findings in a patient who is abusing alcohol but is not intoxicated or in acute withdrawal are: 1. liver disease (a) enlarged liver (b) spider angioma (c) liver palms; 2. oral clues (a) green tongue from breath fresheners (b) brown-coated mouth (c) poor dental hygiene (d) vitamin malnutrition, avitaminosis (e) alcohol on breath; 3. tobacco-stained finger; 4. tremor; 5. tachycardia; 6. night sweats; 7. nystagmus.

In conclusion, many people, men and women, seek release from anxiety, insomnia, depression, or grief, through use of drugs, including alcohol. Although these symptoms may be a part of a psychiatric disorder, they are also part of ordinary living and the value of time taken by the physician for expression of interest and brief reassurance, should not be underestimated. Assessment of the cause of the symptoms is most important, and also finding out what the symptom means to the patient. When symptoms are severe, or prolonged, or interfere with work or personal relationships, treatment may be needed, but the availability of drugs should not eliminate consideration of psychotherapy or improvement of a patient's social or occupational situation. In treating anxiety, a physician should consider alternative treatments, such as relaxation therapy, biofeedback, hypnosis, and other community resources. The use of a psychotropic drug in this context needs to be recognized for what it is—a chemical method of coping with a psychological distress and should be short term. Medicalized addiction to create wellbeing must stop.

The "chemical trap" exists both for patients and for physicians. It is a dangerous one and increasing alarmingly in its prevalence, but awareness can lead to prevention and early recognition of a "trapped victim"—the first step towards a chemical-free, healthy recovery. That, to me, is what medicine is about.

Women Problem Drinkers: Anonymous Alcoholics

by Cheryl Laham

My specialty is the alcoholic woman and I will be referring to her in my speech. However, I think you'll find that what I have to say about her is typical of all drug-dependent women.

Women today are gaining recognition in one area where we didn't have to organize — alcoholism. The number of visible alcoholic women is increasing and yet, the lag in available treatment resources is devastating. I am a community outreach worker for the Women's Alcoholism Program of Cambridge and Somerville, Massachusetts. We are one of 14, federally funded, women's programs, and that number is particularly meagre in comparison to the 547 federally funded other programs of which only 20% are utilized by women.

Why aren't adequate services being developed for the growing number of women alcoholics? Why do alcoholic women go undetected as they pass through the maze of well-meaning friends, doctors' offices, and social agencies? Why aren't women utilizing the few services that are available to them?

The answers to these questions are directly related to the

Ms Laham is community consultant for Women's Alcohol Program of CASPAR (Cambridge and Somerville Program for Alcoholism Rehabilitation) Boston, Mass.

status of the alcoholic woman in our society. She is riddled with stigma and guilt. As an alcoholic woman, she has two strikes against her. As a woman, she's a second class citizen, and, as an alcoholic, she is perceived by many as shameless, immoral, and sexually promiscuous, all of which causes her to seek help from people other than the alcoholism specialist, rather than admit to a disease which is humiliating and over which she feels she has no control.

The Women's Alcoholism Program has believed from the very beginning that outreach is the primary method to bring more women into treatment. Our outreach efforts have been many and varied. They have included radio and television spots; newspaper articles and ads; speaking engagements at women's clubs, rotary clubs, and other local organizations; and two full radio shows. We have held workshops, staffed booths at women's fairs, held conferences, and contributed articles on women and alcoholism to various publications. During the past year, we have formed working and sharing relationships with all parts of the women's community of which we are a part. And we have been principal in setting up various support networks for the alcoholic woman. For instance, there is an organization called Amethyst Women in Boston, which is a support group for lesbian alcoholics and provides them with an alternative to the bars. Amethyst Women holds dances, dinners, and speaker meetings monthly, and we are currently drawing more than 100 women to our events.

Another example of the success of our acceptance by our community is a benefit we held last week. We produced this benefit jointly with Respond, a local organization for battered women and children. The Boston women's music collective, printers, and other groups, donated their time and efforts because they believe in the significance of our work. More than 500 people attended this benefit, the purpose of which was to raise money for a halfway house and further publicize our program.

Awareness of alcoholism as a major problem for women is becoming more widely recognized, both within the community and in the general alcoholism treatment community. Our outreach program has had several different goals:

1) To draw more women into treatment.

2) To reach out to women in earlier stages of alcoholism, given the stigma experienced by alcoholic women, given that it's so great that women are often hidden and protected and come for help at a later, more progressed stage of alcoholism.

3) To develop awareness in the community of the extent of alcoholism as a woman's problem. It is still primarily perceived as a man's disease.

4) To develop awareness of alcoholism resources for women. As the only program for alcoholic women in our community, we serve as a referral and information centre.

5) To stimulate and support the development of additional resources for alcoholic women. There are an estimated 8,000 to 10,000 alcoholic women in our community. We serve approximately 1,000 a year. Our size and staff limitations make it impossible for us to serve all of the alcoholic women in our area.

6) To form links with other women's organizations in our community. Cambridge is known for its steady increase in women's services since the early 1970s. In our neighborhood alone, there are six women's service organizations within a three-block radius. Through collective support, we hope to reach out to more women as well as to serve the women we see in a more comprehensive manner.

7) To educate our community about alcoholism, its detection, and treatment, through alcoholism workshops and training sessions.

Incidentally, when I refer to our community, I'm speaking of our agency of CASPAR, as well as other service organizations. The Women's Alcoholism Program is one unit within a larger alcoholism program of CASPAR, which stands for the Cambridge and Somerville Program for Alcoholism Rebabilitation. CASPAR also includes two detoxification centres, an emergency walk-in service, three men's residences, a dry drop-in centre, an alcohol education project, and an outpatient service. Our outreach is involved in a two-pronged approach. As we have trained outside community agencies about alcoholism, they have, in turn, referred women to us. In order to ensure women will receive relevant treatment within the larger CASPAR program, we felt a necessity to train CASPAR staff on issues for women.

Education

First, I want to focus on the alcohol education we have done with agencies outside of the CASPAR system. Many alcoholic women seek the counsel of family physicians, social workers, psychiatrists, nurses, or non-traditional women's service agencies, long before they even recognize their problem as alcoholism. It has been our experience that very few, if any, helping professionals or people in the counselling community, receive adequate training in alcoholism. The first contact an alcoholic woman often makes in her search for help is with such non-traditional service organizations as health clinics, women's centres, or women's counselling collectives. During our first year, we chose to work with feminist organizations and agencies that serve primarily women because they are too often the last groups to be offered such training from other alcoholism centres. In the past year-and-a-half, my co-worker and I have held alcoholism education workshops with 17 agencies, and trained more than 180 individual staff members. The aim of our contract is to set up six, two-hour sessions, that's a maximum of 12 hours. Yet we must often compromise for less time, sometimes as little as one brief session.

Our strategy in such cases is to accept the time limitation and attempt to convince them of the seriousness of the problem for women and the necessity for more alcoholism training. Because these women's organizations were well versed on women, our emphasis in the training was on alcoholism. They were eager to learn, especially those who had previous contact with alcoholics. They were frustrated and wanted answers. In spite of their varying backgrounds professionally, and their life experiences, participants entered our learning situation with preconceived notions about the alcoholic woman, whether or not they had had personal contact with such a woman.

Their attitudes varied from disgust, to pity, to fear, and regardless of their attitudes, each approached the alcoholic client with a combination of anger, pity, trepidation, and impending frustration.

Edith Gomberg, who is a women researcher and has done various studies on alcoholic women, states that the conscious and unconscious attitudes of the therapist to women and to alcoholics have much more bearing on the outcome of treatment than the techniques used. Therefore, the attitude of the therapist is crucial, if not critical, to the potential recovery of the alcoholic woman. Given that care givers are unable to detect alcoholism, based primarily upon their lack of knowledge and attitudes, our training is designed to focus on these two areas.

I'd like to run through a sample of four sessions that my co-worker and I might do with such a group.

The first session would be on facts and feelings about alcohol and alcoholism. Initially, we would encourage the members to share their own drinking herstories/histories. This is often the first time they've ever had an opportunity to think of their drinking and their drinking patterns. Also, it helps to build their empathy for what it's like for the woman client to speak about such a taboo topic. We define drinking and responsible drinking so that the provider can educate her client to help determine whether or not she's drinking responsibly or alcoholically.

In the second session, we would focus on alcoholism and the alcoholic. We would define alcoholism and introduce an Alcoholics Anonymous speaker. Then we would discuss issues specific to the alcoholic woman.

In the third session, we would discuss alcoholism and its effects on those closest to the alcoholic. In this session we would introduce an Al-Anon speaker and discuss the role of the provider as an educator, a resource provider, and support system for the alcoholic woman.

In the last session, we would talk about treatment. We would discuss danger signals and clues of alcoholism. We would then simulate a roleplay of approaching the woman alcoholic as a client. You'll notice that not until the last session do we deal with approaching the client. Only until the care giver has an understanding of her own biases, plus some factual knowledge about alcoholism and its symptoms, will she be prepared to confront her client.

Lastly, we contract for consultation, which is really follow-up training. Unless care givers have continued contact with alcoholics, they tend to lose the impact of the information received during their training. The consultation that we do is negotiated differently with different agencies. In some cases, it's a case by case consultation. In others, we hold monthly group discussions about different topics on women and alcoholism.

Relevant

Our outreach has resulted in more women coming into our alcoholism program for treatment. In order to offer relevant treatment, our program must be receptive to the unique needs of the alcoholic woman. The CASPAR program has between 90 and 100 employees, and like any other cross-section of society, they share many sexist attitudes. As the newest program to CASPAR, and the only program devoted solely to women, we felt the need to do consciousness raising around sexist attitudes with our own alcoholism staff. We conducted a six-week training series on the alcoholic woman and their responses were very positive. Between 35 and 50 male and female staff members attended each session. We developed various methods in consciousness raising tools for this seminar. It included opinion questionnaires, attitude statements, and surveys. We developed a word association exercise to draw out their stereotypes, not only of men and women, but of women and men alcoholics. We produced a musical selection of songs, depicting different views of women and men over time. We developed a guided experience exercise in which participants explored the feelings of the alcoholic woman from her perspective, beginning with her realization that she has a drinking problem, and concluding with her entry into the emergency walk-in service of CASPAR. Lastly, we wrote a booklet entitled *Issues for Women in Treatment* and developed a video taped roleplay of women in a halfway house which depicts those issues. To stimulate further their sensitivity, we also sponsored follow-up seminars for the CASPAR staff on issues for women, which included the following topics: women's history, the lesbian alcoholic, battered women, and self-help health care.

The growing numbers of women using our treatment services is the most obvious example of the success of our outreach efforts. Prior to the inception of the women's alcoholism program in September of 1975, women accounted for only 10% to 15% of the population using our outpatient services, and fewer than 10% of the patients in detox. By August of 1976, less than one year later, the percentage of women tripled in the outpatient department and doubled in our detox population. In addition, more women coming to our services are in the early stages of alcoholism, or perhaps just beginning to question their drinking. We feel this is a direct result of our outreach efforts.

As the number of women increase and we continue to reach women in early alcoholism or alcohol abuse, the general characteristics of women using our services has broadened. For example, in the past, the majority of women we served were in the middle age range, whereas now the ages are more varied. We are beginning to reach communities of women who have not used CASPAR before. Women as young as 16 have been admitted to our detoxification units. Lesbian women, and feminist and professional women have also entered treatment. A third of the agencies we did alcoholism training with have contracted for follow-up consultation. This has established regular contact and led to several direct referrals. Two new women's alcoholism support groups were organized as a result of our community work, and a third group for elderly women is now being discussed.

What I have attempted to discuss today is a concept of agency outreach as intervention at the first point a woman seeks help. Agency outreach to outside organizations does bring in more women and more types of women. In-service training within alcoholism programs results in staff members being more sensitive to the issues particular to alcoholic women. Only until such sensitivity can be assured, will alcoholic women enter treatment and stay in treatment.

It is up to us, those of us in the field of alcoholism and those in care giving positions, to break the anonymity of the alcoholic woman by providing an informal and informed supportive space for her to discuss her drinking, where the helping professionals —doctors, social workers, nurses, etc.—all play a crucial role in the detection and treatment of the alcoholic woman.

I want to encourage those of you not in the alcoholism field to learn all you can about alcoholism and its effects, and to explore your attitudes about women alcoholics. Can you respect an alcoholic woman? How does it feel to question a woman about her drinking, whether she be a client, a friend, or a relative? Have you ever hesitated to approach a woman client about her drinking? Alcoholism and suicide are both life threatening. If you had a suicidal client, would you avoid talking about suicide with her?

I want to encourage you to use the resources around you, to familiarize yourselves with agencies that serve women, such as the Women's Counselling, Referral and Education Center, and to encourage the continued exploration into the issues of the alcoholic woman at agencies such as The Donwood Institute and the Addiction Research Foundation.

To those of you in the field, I encourage you to explore your attitudes regarding women, and to reach out to the local agencies in your community, where one out of 20 women they serve is alcoholic. Women problem drinkers need not be the anonymous alcoholics that they are today. Only through collective support and effort can we offer alcoholic women a way out of the maze of shame and denial.

Personal Reflections on Women and Alcohol

by Jan DuPlain

Special thanks to all the staff at The Donwood Institute and to the women who have come from different parts of Canada to be here today. It's the first time I've been back to Canada since travelling around the United States seven or eight years ago with a friend in our little Volkswagen. We came to Niagara Falls, Canadian side, trying not to spend any money, and ended up at the local jail for the night so we could complete travelling without spending a cent. That's my memory of Canada. It's good coming back and participating in this conference as a free person.

It's been quite a year for me. I was talking to some women at my table and explained that this is a reflective period for me in terms of what's happening in the United States and around the country on the women and alcoholism issue. Sitting in my hotel room last night and wondering what I could share with you, I looked through different speeches (I've written) and didn't like any. Instead, I'd like to share with you, on a personal level, how I got involved; how the women and alcoholism movement was an issue whose time had come; and how I was in a place of my own growth and involvement in the alcoholism issue and the women's issue that brought me to where I am now.

Ms. DuPlain is executive director, Office on Women, National Council on Alcoholism, Washington, D.C.

I had been living in New York City and was in the final stages of my own alcoholism; I came down to Washington, D.C. to begin my recovery. That first year was the time I learned about alcoholism (our representative from Massachusetts talked about that need at the very beginning of a woman's sobriety).

In the second year, I was watching television one night and heard Gloria Steinem talking about the many women's issues and concerns in the nation. A clock went off in my head; I ran out the next day and bought every book ever written on women's issues. Thus began my personal involvement with women's activities. Specifically an organization called NOW, the National Organization for Women.

I attended consciousness raising groups and began to get a sense of what was taking place in my own life, my own recovery, and the need for me to connect with other women. The real turning point in my recovery began when I connected with other women, helping other women. That, to me, is when the real growth started. I became involved in the women's community and went through what many of you might have experienced; I began a very hostile period; I was very sensitive to everything I heard; and I was standing on my soapbox attacking everyone. As a result, I wasn't getting my points across, I was irritating many people, and I wasn't included in many things. I had to go through this period and I know many women do and (some) are right now.

The third stage was kind of a mellowing period. A woman friend said: "Jan, do you want to be *heard* or do you want to *change* things?" That stuck somehow. Did I want to be heard? Did I want to change things? I meditated on that and realized the way I was going about things might not be the best way. I did want to change things, and I did want to reach out to other women.

I was working as public relations director of a well-known theatre in Washington, D.C. and got involved with a local council on alcoholism; I got more involved with them and less with theatre. Doors opened and about 4½ years after my recovery from alcoholism began, I was offered a job with the National Clearinghouse for Alcohol Information. They knew I

74

was interested in women's issues and of my personal commitment to the alcoholism field. I was covering the northeast region, which included 16 states, and addressed the women and alcoholism issue in these states.

In 1975, during International Women's Year, there was a growing interest throughout the country in women's issues. This permitted the alcoholism field, and gave myself and others an opportunity, to talk with State alcohol directors about what they were doing for women alcoholics. I think it was time for everyone where that issue was a big concern. The response in each state was, yes! they were interested, and yes! they would like to see a Task Force in their area to look at the needs and concerns of the woman alcoholic. In each place, they didn't have halfway houses for women; there were outreach problems (for getting women into treatment); child care issues; vocational rehabilitation issues (women were oftentimes given sewing and basket weaving); nine out of 10 women alcoholics would be left by their husbands and would need career counselling. These were the issues that were discussed.

At the end of that year, I attended a conference in Miami — the First National Conference on Women, Alcohol, and Drugs. I met other women from national organizations who were beginning women's alcohol and drug coalitions. It was an exciting moment for us to hear about what was happening around the country on this issue. I returned to Washington, D.C. and spoke with the National Council on Alcoholism (NCA), the largest voluntary health organization in the country, and revealed that the Women and Alcoholism constituency was growing quickly and needed a base for leadership to bring these issues together. I talked to NCA in November: in March, 1976, the board established the first National Office on Women.

NCA was started by a woman named Marty Mann, one of the first women in Alcoholics Anonymous, and the first woman publicly recognized as a recovered woman alcoholic. Marty told me about her dream when she founded the National Council. It was to go through women's organizations and talk to them about the issue of alcoholism — but the doors were closed. It was too threatening an issue. They said they didn't have any women alcoholics, or any problems with alcoholism. It was a dream come true for Marty, to see this National Office on Women open and see women in our community taking on this issue of alcoholism.

During International Women's Year, there had been many women's issues presented — abortion, ERA (Equal Rights Amendment), employment, you name it. The one issue that wasn't brought up and wasn't looked upon as a women's issue was alcoholism. If the women and alcoholism concern was going to be a national concern, we had to have the support of our sisters from the women's community. So, when we opened the office, NCA held their first annual conference and we had, for the first time, a women and alcoholism tract. Women's organizations all over the United States joined us. This issue was an issue that all women could come together on; one that would transcend issues of politics, economics, and social concerns. When you're reaching out to a woman alcoholic, you don't ask whether she works in the home or in the office. This was an issue that transcended all issues. The response from the women's community was absolutely incredible. Business and professional women, junior leagues, conservative groups, activist and militant groups came forth from all over the country to come to this conference. Our theme, *Women unite to combat alcoholism: an interchange of ideas* was a reality.

We saw the first Congress of State Task Forces. Task Forces from the hills and the countryside came together for the first time. We had a *Roll Call of the States:* it was like a political convention. We started with Alabama and Arkansas, and California, each one sharing what they were doing about women and alcoholism in their states; what was not going on; what were some of the needs. All the groups had felt so isolated and there was tremendous excitement in the room as they heard from each of the states that they too, were involved in this issue.

Soon after that, we contacted Rutgers Summer School of Alcohol Studies, the oldest summer school within the United States. We told them there was a massive constituency of concern and the time had come for them to initiate a course on women and alcoholism. They did, and we held the first course on women and alcoholism. Women and men from more than 70 states came together and we brought in different speakers.

Events kept mushrooming—the issue was hot. A friend of Dr. Susan B. Anthony, the grand niece and namesake of the famous suffragette, gave me her copy of the book *Survival Kit,* by Susan, and said it might well be the most important book I would ever read. I looked at it and said: "You mean she's alive?" They said, she's alive and living in Miami.

I contacted Susan, and we talked, and I asked her if she could come to Washington. She was at a period in her life where she had just turned 60 years old, was in her 30th year of continuous sobriety as a recovered alcoholic, and was going to celebrate the 56th anniversary of the 19th Amendment (or the Anthony Amendment) which gave women the right to vote. All three things were coming together, and I thought this would be the perfect time to hold a special event on Capitol Hill, giving visibility to the woman alcoholic. I brought her to Washington and we co-sponsored a special reception with Senator William Hathaway, chairman of the subcommittee on narcotics and alcoholism. The press responded enthusiastically. It was the first time Dr. Anthony had publicly shared the story of her recovery as an alcoholic.

At that reception, Senator Hathaway said publicly to the newspapers that it was time to hold Congressional Hearings on Women and Alcoholism; there was massive concern nationally around this issue. A month later, we held the first Congressional Hearings ever in our history on women and alcoholism; women from different professions, and recovered women alcoholics, came to Washington to give statements.

At that moment, we validated our concern. This was truly something that was here to stay. We had the credibility and interest that would solidify the movement. We're now in Phase II of this concern. I've been from state to state, speaking at different conferences and workshops, and am in a reflective period in terms of my involvement with the field. I've gone to more than 25 states and been involved in 50 workshops and conferences in the last year. So I'm pretty tired.

One of the most exciting things that happened was with the Air Force. They liked a women and alcoholism course we put together and sent me to the Phillipines and to Germany to speak to Air Force counsellors working in alcoholism.

The Phase II we're in now is that we've developed the constituency, the Task Forces, but we need to put together a women and alcoholism agenda, listing what our national objectives are, and come forth as a national voice. At the last NCA forum in San Diego (May, 1977), we began the First National Women and Alcoholism agenda, including issues on prevention, education, training, occupational, legislative, the media, halfway houses, the other victims of alcoholism. Our keynote speaker, Ruth Abram, executive director of The Women's Action Alliance (which is the first voluntary women's coalition that's been put together in the United States and includes more than one hundred women's organizations) spoke about an alliance between the women's organizations and the alcoholism and women's movement.

The force that it needed was the blending of these two groups, women's organizations with the alcoholism and women constituency. This is the long term impetus and permanency we need to sustain ourselves. When we first opened the office it was a showpiece. It's much more than a showpiece now. It's taken on great strength and made great strides.

That's an overview, my involvement in the magnitude of concern that has taken place the last two years. It blossomed very fast.

The next event is the First National Leadership Training Institute on Women and Alcoholism in Washington, D.C. (October, 1977). We're going to bring in State task force representatives from around the country for a four-day intensive sharing of programs and projects in their states; we're planning to meet national alcoholism leaders, legislators, and press club members. Last year in Washington, and this year in California, NCA held a banquet called Operation Understanding, where well-known personalities from all over the United States came together to announce their recovery from alcoholism to the press and to the world. It's my belief that as more women who have recovered from the disease of alcoholism share their recovery with others, the stigma and lack of understanding about alcoholism will begin to break down. In many parts of the United States, and in the world, alcoholism is looked upon as a moral issue and not as a health issue. When it comes to the woman alcoholic, if you are looking at it in terms of a moral issue, there's the double standard for her. A banquet which brings women together to share their own alcoholism will help break the stigma.

My own involvement is taking a different turn these next six months. Not only did all of this happen professionally but I got married (much to the horror of my friends and much to my delight). But, having been a single woman for 34 years, it was quite an adjustment. Talk about an identity change. Not only did I get married, but I acquired a 12-year-old son. You never know what's unfolding for you. It added a whole new dimension in terms of my involvement with the field and, also, a new dimension in terms of understanding women's issues in general. I called my mother and said: "I have a new understanding for married women." She laughed. She's seen me go through different stages and she enjoys it.

We talked today about a lot of these issues—about women, that we're not a homogeneous group, that we don't have one solid voice, that we come from such different backgrounds, and that we're at different stages of our development.

The one thing that I think is important for all of us, is to respect whatever place we're in; not to feel threatened by the place that others are at; and to support each other where we're at.

The women's movement has had some devisiveness, it split groups from groups. I think that was the way the press has covered the movement. The women and alcoholism issue is throwing the net very wide and bringing in women from different backgrounds, different stages of development, and of personal growth. Let's respect and support each other. Margaret Mead and others speak about the need for women to help and reach out for other women. I think each new thing that's happened to me personally has brought me to a new level of understanding. When I first opened the office, a lot of direction, for example, was focused just on the women alcoholics; then I met Josie Couture who was developing a national constituency for "the other victims of alcoholism" and she opened my sights to the other person, the other victim. So often that person was looked upon only in relationship to the alcoholic. Josie Couture said there was a need to look at the other people affected—at treatment, research, prevention, and education, whether or not the alcoholic got help. She provided another dimension for me in terms of our office and travels; we're looking not only at the woman alcoholic, but other women affected by alcoholism.

It's a marvellous day for this particular conference to take place. I know I was listed to discuss Trends in Treatment but as I listened to the women speaking beautifully, eloquently, this morning, the issues are the same ones we're discussing in the United States. In my room last night, and today, I thought I would instead share my involvement, the growth of the movement as it's developed in the U.S.A. The treatment discussed this morning and this afternoon will touch every aspect of it.

It's 2 o'clock and I would like to wrap this up. When I arrived at the Canadian (Toronto) airport last night, I looked through the gift section and the different post cards. There were two I liked especially. They seemed very appropriate in terms of what's gone on in my life and the movement itself: "You have helped me in my work and in myself, and I have helped you in your work and in yourself, and I'm grateful to heaven for this—you and me."

That's the field, and the personal development of the women and alcoholism movement. The interest in women and alcoholism is mushrooming and will go on mushrooming. My place is moving in another direction—more reflective, more meditative, moving out of the action part.

My feelings are described in a poem by Frank Dickey: "If I had my life to live over, I would relax more. I wouldn't take so many things so seriously. I would take more chances. I would climb more mountains and swim more rivers. Next time I'd start bare-footed earlier in the Spring and stay that way later in the Fall. I wouldn't make such good grades unless I enjoyed working for them. I'd go to more dances. I'd ride on more merry-go-rounds. I'd pick more daisies."

The great joy of living is that there are new times for you and me that can open that door to a new place we want to go. Life is a series of new lives. I've enjoyed being with you today. Thanks for letting me spend this reflective period of my life with you.

80

Feminist Counselling: New Directions for Women

by Helen Levine

I came to feminist counselling by way of attempting to combine my experience and skills as social worker with my awareness and experience as woman. It began as an attempt to translate into practice changing perceptions of myself and other women in this society.

As with most of us, this development did not arise apart from crises in my own life. I am and have been a consumer of mental health services, both in and out of hospital. I have been on both sides of the institution, as provider and consumer, at different times in my life. By now, it seems pointless to write or speak in safe generalities when my own situation has had such a profound impact on how I perceive myself and others, either as provider or consumer of service. In the name of professionalism or normalcy or whatever, most social workers have developed and used personal masks and images in practice. My contention is that this has hindered the helping process; created a phony social distance between providers and consumers, and a lack of the very humanity we would like to think we value.

Ms Levine teaches a course on women and social work at the school of social work, Carleton University, Ottawa. She gave an informal presentation based on this article, Feminist Counselling: A Look at New Possibilities, which was originally published in 76 and Beyond: A Woman's Issue of The Social Worker, Summer, 1976.

I find it useful to preface my comments on feminist counselling with a necessarily brief commentary of two issues:

1) The artificial separation in our lives between the public and private spheres, or, as referred to by the women's movement, the personal, and political.

For women, this has meant being primarily responsible for the personal and private realm of the family and being denied serious involvement in the decision-making, leadership, and power positions that determine the direction of our society. It has meant being a 52% majority holding minority status and playing a secondary service role in family and job ghettos.

The public and private spheres of life are desperately in need of fusion if we are to attain the full and equal status denied us to date. Thus, the emphasis in the contemporary women's movement to help weave the personal and political, or family and societal aspects into a unified whole.

2) Critical features of traditional practice that I think have created, rather than resolved, problem areas for the consumer of service.

I see the use of the medical model, with its "case" approach, and its "treatment" emphasis, as counterproductive; and sometimes a means of enhancing the ego of the practitioner whilst further reducing that of the consumer. Treatment in itself, derived from medicine, is a "disease" concept and from this perspective has grown an emphasis on pathology, labelling, diagnosis, and, in the end, stigma. It is clearly no accident, given this perspective, that consumers (individuals or groups) are inclined to privatize their experiences of receiving help. The privatization, in turn, frequently adds to the problem.

There is, in traditional counselling, directly or indirectly, an emphasis on individual personal inadequacy and individual personal adjustment. Conversely, there is frequently an avoidance of political awareness and involvement on the part of the practitioner, by way of reorganizing and/or attempting to change those "norms", social conditions, or societal institutions that social workers know wreak havoc with people's lives. Practitioners often have a stronger vested interest in professionalism and career advancement than in the fate of the consumer. Social workers, along with other "helping professions," play a role by mystifying consumers, the public—and sometimes ourselves—with jargon, status, and expertise.

We work in hierarchical institutions, work settings where leadership and decision-making positions, in once a women's profession, have been consistently shifting to men—take a glance at the federal government departments, Children's Aid Societies and Schools of Social Work. This, despite the window dressing of International Women's Year and the outpouring of studies regarding women in and out of social work; which clearly illustrate the rampant discrimination practices against women.

Feminist counselling

The idea of non-sexist counselling help for women is not particularly new. There are, or have been, women's counselling collectives in Toronto, Montreal, and elsewhere in Canada. This kind of service has grown out of the women's movement, and was given added impetus by Betty Friedan's *Feminine Mystique* and Phyllis Chesler's *Women and Madness.* For me, feminist counselling challenges the frequent premise in the provision of services that "more of the same is better," and states decisively that more of the same would be more of a disaster for women.

Feminist counselling deals with sexism at the heart of its rationale, with the clear implication that services planned, designed, and often delivered by men in authoritative positions, have frequently done incalculable harm to women. The question is how to offer women something other than the sexist, chemical, adjustment-oriented service that passes for help—something instead involving mutual assistance, support, and a new "vision of the possible."

One word of caution—people say to me: "What exactly is feminist counselling?" I have no absolute answer or blueprint. What I do know, and have practiced, is a helping process that means working with women, individually or in groups, around their life situations *as related* to the society that has shaped them. It has to do with a "vision of the possible," out of our own oppression, and involving our own potential. It is no mysterious, professional technique.

Many of the ingredients that go into feminist counselling are not new. But given professionalism in the 20th century, with its emphasis on pathology, on a sexist double standard of normalcy for men and women, and on turning the victim of oppression into the problem, some of the old truths need to be learned anew.

One of the questions to be asked is counselling by whom, with whom and with what purposes in mind. In a sexist society, by women counsellors, I would say. Not all women qualify because many have clearly adopted the values of a male-dominated society; but women with life experience, commitment, and skills. The order is *not* accidental—women who recognize sexism and its personal and political consequences, and are actively seeking change for themselves and others from this perspective. There are a few exceptional men who qualify as helping people for women, but, by and large, their record as helpers of women has been a dismal failure.

I am often asked: "Isn't feminist counselling just good counselling?" My answer is a firm no. Feminist counselling is intrinsically different and these are some of the differences I have identified:

1. I call myself a feminist counsellor to state my own position clearly. A consumer looking for help has a right to know the bias or the ideology of the practitioner, clearly and explicitly. All practitioners have a bias, consciously or unconsciously, and potential consumers should have some personal information before they begin to use the helper.

    A first session usually has to do with sharing information about one another. I need to know what the problem is and if I can help; the consumer needs to be free to ask how I work, to explore my attitudes and experience, to check out such facts as she may deem important—if I have children, if I have worked inside and/or outside the home, if I am divorced, etc. There is no neutral ground here, just two people exploring whether one can help the other.

2. Does feminist counselling mean imposing an ideology on others? I think not. For me, it means sharing my experience and my view of women's place in the world *when* it seems relevant, *when* it pertains to the consumer's life struggles, or when aspects of my own life may be helpful regarding the issue at hand. Consumers of feminist counselling may or may not move into or out of the women's movement, into or out of politics, into or out of marriage. That is a personal decision to be made with full knowledge of costs and benefits, and with the advantage in feminist counselling of not having oppressive societal norms reinforced about what women should or should not be.

3. A feminist counsellor uses her own life experience, her sorrows and joys, her traumas and learning if relevant to the consumer's life situation. It is a peer kind of relationship. The sharing helps to demystify the counsellor as omnipotent professional and truly to universalize, in a visible and concrete way, the struggle of human beings to survive and to change.

4. No formal assessment, diagnosis, or treatment is involved. One central assumption of feminist counselling is that "individuals' problems are not viewed as individual pathology, but as a manifestation of social disorganization." It is understood that chronic responses of guilt, self-blame, and depression are built into the societal structure of a woman's life. This approach does not deny the validity of one woman's personal pain and her need to express that individual hurt as she chooses to or needs to, but the roots of her fear and pain and anger are recognized, and then in time, may be translated into some form of personal and/or political action—from passive, helpless pain to active, hopeful struggle, from dependent acceptance to independent assertion, at whatever level and whatever pace the person chooses or can handle.

5. A recognition of the need for achievement and involvement in society at large. Though men verbally glorify women's roles in the home, they seldom wish to exchange. Women, on the other hand, often need and want the ego and self esteem that comes of work or achievement beyond the home, in the public sphere. Being Somebody's wife or Somebody's girlfriend or Somebody's mother negates a woman's ego. Hans Selye has recognized that universal and basic human need to care for the self. Men recognize it for themselves, women are not supposed to have it. A feminist counsellor will recognize this basic human need in women and encourage its development.

6. Fees are geared to income. No OHIP coverage and a current maximum of $15.00, or free. It is not a highly commercial undertaking. People usually meet in an informal, quiet, and personalized setting. It takes away from the usual institutional aura that helps make people feel abnormal and sick. Most often, it significantly reduces the psychological distance and barrier created by desks in sterile offices.

7. An underlying assumption of feminist counselling is that women have strength, potential, and the will to change their situations, *especially in concert with other women*. It is recognized that many women suffer from that curse of minority groups, low self-esteem, and that this reflects societal distortions perpetrated on people. Certainly women do *not* need male, sexist, authority figures to reinforce their low self-esteem. We need other women and society in general to recognize and reinforce our strengths, to nurture our confidence.

8. Women often have difficulty in truly acknowledging, to self and others, the depth of our sense of inadequacy in this patriarchal society. Trained to pretence, we need help from feminist counselling in asserting our mix of strength and weakness as part of each human existence.

9. Feminist counselling recognizes that women are especially deprived of nurturance. Traditionally, we do the nurturing, the entertaining, the nursing, the appointment keeping, the

understanding, the child care, the worrying that is all part of the sex role stereotype. The fact is that women need "wives"—meaning reverse nurturing. Instead of helping a woman to accept the nurturant role, the counsellor helps her, and sometimes a family, to recognize her central and essential needs as a person. The consumer is not seen as adjunct to family, but as a separate person, in relationship to others in her world.

10. There is an absence of jargon, of professional mystification, or mechanistic techniques used with the consumer. There is a presence of simplicity, clarity and sharing, with the simple acknowledgement that the consumer, at this point in time, needs help. It may be the provider who at some other point in time has been or will be the consumer and this is made explicit.

11. A feminist counsellor knows a woman's loneliness in a personal and political sense. She understands, as men cannot, the risks involved in staying in a nuclear family or leaving, in being a single parent with children, in being on welfare, or in a job ghetto. A feminist counsellor knows well the isolation of women, one from the other, with husband or male friend often the main point of reference. She recognizes a woman's need for a network of support and services, not traditionally provided by society, but beginning to emerge from the women's movement.

12. A feminist counsellor usually finds it most helpful to work collectively, both at a personal and/or political level. Women learn from one another, from sharing lives they have been taught to keep private, from finding new ways of tackling the struggle. The feminist counsellor may have been a member of a consciousness raising group and/or other women's action groups herself. Her helping thus derives from relevant personal experience as well as work outside the home or narrowly defined political action.

13. A feminist counsellor shares information and knowledge with the consumer, recognizing it may be vital in dealing with the problem at hand, i.e., WOW, a handbook for women on welfare. Literature relevant to women's particu-

lar needs is often most helpful and usually well known to the feminist counsellor. There is an underlying recognition that knowledge is power, and must be shared.

14. The feminist counsellor knows the newly developing, ever-changing services for women in the community. She knows them from the inside as part of the women's movement. So instead, for example, of referring a woman to "Manpower", she may refer her to a Women's Career Counselling Service. It is often a personal referral to known people in Women's Centres, C.R. Groups, Interval Houses, Women's Studies Courses, Women's Career Counselling, Rape Crisis Centres, etc.

15. Assertiveness training is sometimes used by feminist counsellors to help women recognize and lay claim to their civil and personal rights. Women are traditionally taught to submit and conform, not to demand and protest, so confidence and assertion must grow in a central way if things are to change. Role-playing is one interesting form of assertiveness training and can deal with past or current situations, large and small. Such situations as demanding time and quality care from a doctor, re-arranging domestic chores with one's mate, laying claim to equal pay for work of equal value, joining a union, working out a relationship with mother, father, or child, etc.

It is true that many of the factors I have mentioned *may* also be part of good counselling. However, who it is done by and with will transmit attitudes and value systems, consciously or unconsciously, that nurture or deny the objectives noted.

It is in relation to the family and to politics and ideology that feminist counselling reflects major differences. I would like to underline the centrality of the nuclear family structure in our society as an institution which has been used as a particularly effective vehicle in the oppression of women. It is also the institution that many helping professions strive to uphold in its traditional outlines, no matter what the cost to women in the process.

It may be of passing interest to the reader to know that I have for some time been using this kind of material on feminist counselling and its origins in my own case comfortably within the women's movement. Not so within social work. "Why?", I mused recently. In the end it appeared that my caution was directly related to a lack of confidence in the capacity of many social workers to appreciate and to accept (not tolerate) the focus on women as well as the implications of a psychiatric hospitalization. I guessed—correctly I think—that my credibility as person and as social worker would likely be endangered by my making known the fact of being an ardent feminist and a consumer of service. Ex-patients are usually advised not to disclose a psychiatric hospitalization in the search for employment in social work or elsewhere. Given the continuing stigma, in and out of the helping professions, the essence of survival is to remain a "closet" patient.

Interest in feminism, in women's liberation, even in recognizing women as a majority "minority" requiring new perspectives and new services is most often seen as handicap rather than asset in the practice of social work. I would counter-propose the possibility that being consumer and feminist has provided me with a basic dimension that is potentially invaluable to the practice of social work.

As consumer, I have learned how very limited my perceptions and actions were as a provider of service, and how much I and others must learn, in an ongoing way, from consumers. The following quote perhaps best sums up my own point of view:

> *Consumers are making the point with increased stridency that "human" services are not human, that they are illconceived, that they are palliative fragments designed by those with biased frames of reference who lack sufficient knowledge about the users, and that history reveals their failure. Consumers are questioning the nature and form of services; they are questioning the arrogance of the providers; and they are questioning the professionals' competence. These "Who says so?" questions attack doctors' control over health systems, teachers' control over parents in educational systems, and social workers' control over clients in social service systems."*

Women are the most numerous users of health and social service programs. This is no accident, given the stunted growth patterns and life experience that women are slotted into. If social work is to facilitate effectively personal and/or social change for women, it must begin to address seriously the double standard of employment, health, parenting, and most other aspects of women's lives.

That is what feminist counselling, in a beginning way, is all about.

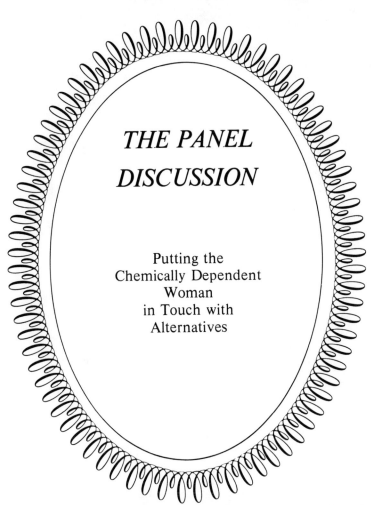

THE PANEL
DISCUSSION

Putting the
Chemically Dependent
Woman
in Touch with
Alternatives

Once the woman with an alcohol/drug problem has been identified, what are her options? A panel discussion — Putting the Chemically Dependent Woman in Touch with Alternatives — offered some suggestions.

Moderator:

Lavada Pinder

Speakers:

Lee Arima

I'm going to outline what the Donwood treatment program is about, its structure, and give you a little information that I hope will help you to decide whether this is the appropriate place for you to refer women and other people you have with addiction problems.

The Donwood is a two-year treatment program. We divide that two years into three phases. We have a day clinic which can handle 24 patients per month, and an inpatient facility which has 49 beds.

Referrals are made by calling our admissions officer, who will arrange a pre-admission interview with one of our doctors, for those who are within reasonable commuting distance. If the person is too far away for that to be feasible, we ask them to have a medical report sent by their family physician so that we can have some indication of their suitability for our program as far as their physical health is concerned. The decision as to whether a person would go into the day clinic, or the inpatient facility, is made at the pre-admission interview.

We have some criteria we like to look at and we don't like to leave that decision up to the referring person. For instance, often a woman or a man will feel he/she wants to be in the day clinic and go home at night to get housework or office work done. We would like to discourage that. We would like people to be able to focus on the program and not be trying to carry on "business as usual" outside. Once people have been accepted into the program, they go on the waiting list and may have to wait for about six to eight weeks for a bed.

Phase I of the two-year program is the first week and consists of detoxification, if necessary, done through relaxation,

Ms Arima is a staff psychologist at The Donwood Institute, Toronto.

training, lots of tender loving care, and lots of support. We give some anticonvulsant medication. If necessary, we may give some tranquillizers for the first few days but our goal is to have people completely withdrawn from chemicals by the time they enter our program. During this phase, the patient is assessed medically, psychologically, and socially, so staff will have an idea where the problems are in each of these different areas for each particular individual. There is time in this week for orientation to the program; we tell people what the program is about, what our expectations are of them, and what they can expect from us. At the end of the first week, there's an intake staff meeting at which all this information is shared and it is decided whether the person is ready now to go on to Phase II of the program, or whether more time is needed in Phase I. The patient would also be introduced to the daily use of Antabuse® or Temposil® during this week.

Phase II of the program consists of the next three weeks, and in this phase we expose the patient to an education in alcoholism. We do this by means of films, video tapes, and discussions. We try to acquaint them with the factors that contribute to the development of an addiction; the changes that take place physically, mentally, and socially with increasing use of chemicals; and the kinds of breakdown that occur. We ask them to look at themselves and see where they fit into all this and become a little clearer about what has been happening to them, and through increased understanding become able to take the necessary steps toward recovery.

We have a nutritionist on staff who, through videos, discussion, and individual consultation, where appropriate, gives people the nutritional information they need to help themselves stay healthy and change their eating patterns.

We have the patient participate in an exercise program and training in relaxation which is done by the physiotherapy department. The physiotherapists give them any extra help they may need in order to relieve their stress and tension, such as hot packs and massage. They are taught techniques to handle stress and keep it in manageable proportions, rather than resorting to use of chemicals.

We have group therapy for our people. Everyone goes into

94

group therapy and they have about 26 hours of group therapy during the time they are at Donwood. Here we try to do a lot of things. We realize that, in that short period of time, we can only make a beginning, maybe only open the door a little bit for people to look in and see what's going on, both inside themselves and around them; see how these things are interacting; where they can make changes; where they can't make changes; and whether the changes need to be changes within themselves or outside. Is there anything they can change about their environment? There is also a drug group for people who are cross-addicted, which meets three times a week. This is in addition to the regular program.

During the last week of Phase II, they begin to do their own personal planning for recovery and to look at the steps they have to take in all areas — the physical, the social, and the emotional — to facilitate their recovery. They look at the problems they have to deal with, how they can deal with them and where they can find the resources to help them. That's Phase II.

Phase III is the next two years and, formally, this consists of weekly meetings in which the alumni come and bring their spouses. We encourage spouse participation. They see it as a family problem and we feel everyone needs to change, not just the identified patient. The family must also be willing to change. Everybody's become a little sick from these chemicals and everybody needs to recover.

We maintain a weekly mail contact with all graduates, and telephone contact with local graduates. This is done by a group of volunteers. We have 52 volunteers from the community, without whom our form of continuing therapy really could not function. The nurse counsellor, as a staff member, maintains contact as well, and is available to the patient. The patient and family members are encouraged to call and let us know if they run into difficulties, to let us know if they're getting uptight, so they come in and talk to us. We can try and sort out what's going on, what can they do, what can we do, where can they find appropriate help. Also, during this period of time, we make appropriate referrals for particular problems to community resources or to resources on our staff.

All the Donwood social activities, and there are many of

them, are available to the alumni during this two-year period. They can come back and get more exposure to exercise and relaxation from the physios; if they're getting into trouble, they don't have to wait 'til they drink. If they do drink, they don't have to come back into hospital. We can help them get back on the rails while they're still in the community. We have a family education program. Weekly, we run a 3½ day program for the families of our patients. We encourage them to come. It's aimed again at providing the families with the same information we provide to the patients and, also, giving the families an opportunity to look at their own personal probelms and feelings, and to do some planning for their own recovery. We also have a teenage program three times a year. This is for the teenage children of our patients and any other teenage children interested in coming. We try to give them an opportunity to understand alcoholism and how it's affected their lives, and to share some of their experiences with other kids, so they don't have to feel so isolated and strange and weird.

Now, I don't want to go on too long. When I was asked to do this, I wondered if I'd have anything to say, and now it looks like I may go on forever, and I don't want to do that. People said to me, be sure to tell everybody about the women's group and what Donwood's got especially for women. And I find that hard to put into words. I think there's an atmosphere at Donwood that contributes to good mental health. I think all our staff are aware of the needs that women have and the issues facing women. I'm not saying we're all 100% and we know all there is to know, but we're aware and we work in that direction. We're not limited in the numbers of women we can take. We don't have two beds allotted or three beds allotted. We can take them as they apply to us. But since the program is oriented towards health and personal growth, we're not trying to fit people into slots. I think, too, on the part of the staff, there's a meeting of our patients as human beings, as people like us who have maybe a different solution to problems, but may be experiencing the same problems we are, and we want to share with them what we know of more effective ways of handling their problems. I don't like the term "coping" too well, because it means to me, sort of just getting by. I want people to do more than cope. I want them to be able to handle things.

I've been asked: "What goes on in your women's group?" I've been asked that by staff at Donwood, and I've been asked that in other places, and I have a hard time putting that into words too. Someone this morning asked: "Is it a consciousness raising group?" Well, I don't call it that. And some people say: "Is it a therapy group?" And the answer to that is, not always.

What we do is, we deal with what's coming up. And it's a mixed group. It's alcoholics and non-alcoholics. And some weeks we're dealing with crises. Somebody's got a crisis on her hands, her husband walked out, or he walked in, or she had a problem with the kids, or she's in a panic state over something. So we deal with that. We try and help her, as a group, by sharing our experiences with her, help her develop some confidence in her own strength, that she can deal with it, that she doesn't need to reach for something else, that there are resources within her that she can use to deal with it. So we deal with crisis and sometimes we deal with consciousness raising because we look at the attitudes, and the way of handling things, and look at that in terms of how they've been programmed into it, and how, as Helen (Levine) mentioned, they're punishing themselves: they don't need anybody to lay it on them, they're laying it on themselves, and how they can help themselves to get out of that pattern. Sometimes we have time to do some therapy when there isn't a crisis going on and a lot of people look into themselves and understand themselves more effectively.

So, I guess the answer is that the group is whatever it needs to be at the particular moment. I think what the women are getting from the group, and what I'm getting from the group, is that we're learning that our feelings are not inappropriate. We're learning that if we're angry, it may not be comfortable, but it may make sense. We're learning that if we're depressed, it may not be because we're crazy. Not that it's okay in the sense that it feels good, but that it doesn't mean we need to be institutionalized somewhere, or that we need to be given pills, or that we need to turn to alcohol. We learn it's all right to feel good things and bad things. I think the women are finding their feelings are not unique and I think it's important the group is mixed because the women who have had an alcohol problem, and the women who have not had an alcohol problem, are finding they have a lot more in common than they have differences, and I think that's a strength for them.

Many of these women in the group have been isolated from other women. They've been isolated from other people. They have no women in their lives that they've been intimate with, in an emotional sense; that they've been able to share themselves with. So they thought their feelings were peculiar and they were less as people and less as women, and that they were unique. And I think they gain strength from seeing that that's not true. I think there's a beginning of trust of other women that takes place as they begin to share. They begin to see other women as resources. Many of them, with their sense of helplessness, have felt the answers could come, should come, must come from their husbands or from men in the community, and they've tended not to look to other women, and I guess we've been programmed somewhat to compete with other women. Now, they're beginning to find that they can trust other women, that other women can be a resource. I think when they see that, they begin to feel better about themselves as women, to know that women can be strong, that women can be all things that a healthy human being needs to be.

Ah, what else? Maybe I'll quit there and if you have any questions later, you can ask me. Now I'll hand it over to Ann (Cools).

Ann Cools

I work in social services. My perspective tends to be that of social service delivery and I would like to say that whenever I come to a meeting about women, on the problems of women, I experience a peculiar kind and quality of pain and frustration because, as women, we seem to be trapped in the personal. And I go home after every meeting and suffer.

As a person involved in social services, I am going to begin by quoting Gustave Flaubert, who wrote *Emma Bovary*. Emma Bovary is pregnant at this time—the quotation goes as follows:

"She hopes for a son. She would name him George. In this way, by delivering a son, she would take revenge for all her female impotence."

I think the problem of dependency is a function, really, of impotence. I love this particular quotation because it articulates the helplessness of women. The term impotence is traditionally a male term, but that is what we are talking about, female impotence, female helplessness. I am sympathetic and very compassionate to this. I would dedicate all my energies to struggling with this, but I am afraid it is what we are talking about.

Now, Women In Transition, as described in the social service network, is an innovative social service. Innovative is a very important word, very important, because if we know anything about social services, we discover very quickly that social services, as a delivery network, has completely ignored women. It holds the view that most of society shares, which is that a woman's place is in the home—inert, inactive, and rotting. I have some very, very definite views on some of these subjects and, I assure you, I do not see the role of the housewife as a

Ms Cools is director of Women In Transition, Toronto.

happy and satisfying one. I see it as tension-riddled, stressed, inactive, encouraging obesity and alcohol use, and as reinforcing dependency.

The specific service that Women In Transition provides is that of addressing the needs of the woman who has been battered, i.e. domestic violence. I completely agree with those who say that, like alcoholism, many of the problems that afflict women have been cast in an air of morality. There has been a camouflage of morality. It is my view that the time has come for us to examine the stress created within the psyche and personality of women as a result of unhappy marital relationships.

The stress, which results from inadequate communications and breakdown of love, is one which social services attend to. Women In Transition is an emergency shelter. The primary service we provide for women is accommodation. We must understand very clearly that when we are dealing with women who are married, and homebound, we are dealing with women who essentially have no independent source of income. This may be quite tolerable and blissful, so long as the marital relationship is harmonious and positive. At the point of marital breakdown, however, particularly if violence on the part of the husband enters the situation, that particular fact—lack of money—becomes intolerable. Objectively, the woman is penniless, without resources, without a place or a friend to turn to. The woman has no options. This is augmented by the fact that, invariably, she has two or three young children who prohibit her physical movement and activity. Our services, therefore, attempt to help women in these circumstances.

There are several issues that we are involved in and concerned with which must be addressed. One of these is an adequate and profound definition of feminist counselling. The problem of dependency is very manifest in the plight of the battered woman. There is an affection for some object, in this instance the husband. There is a profound understanding that this attachment is unhealthy, dangerous, and harmful. Yet, somehow, that information and understanding is quickly forgotten at particular moments in time, the same way as the alcoholic reaches for a drink, or a drug addict for a drug. This is

100

something I am grappling with and profoundly trying to grasp and comprehend. We must seek to understand the fragility and vulnerability of women.

I am going to talk about dependency, and chemical dependency. My view of dependency is essentially that dependency is a characteristic of the female of the species, that is of women. There seems to be a natural tendency in women towards dependency. Each and every one of us has to struggle with it. It seems to me, therefore, that it is only logical that all other dependencies are natural corollaries of that dependency. Women are dependent. Whether they resort to a man, drugs, alcohol, or to a boss. This dependency is rooted in the need for other-directedness. It seems to me we should be very sensitive to the fact that women reach out for objects which satisfy. I quite understand the dynamics at work, where women, in moments of upset, anxiety, or unhappiness, reach out to take hold of other-directedness. In reaching out to a third party, whether it be a doctor, a psychiatrist, a bottle of alcohol, or a pill, or even a cigarette, the point is that she is reaching out for that other-directiveness. This is a dynamic which I personally feel a great concern about and a willingness to work with women in order to overcome it.

I shall now attempt to talk a little about the women we see and assist. I would like to caution, if possible, against generalizing concerning women. We tend to do it when we talk about women, but in truth, and in fact, we are talking about the women who are our peers and within our peer group. We are talking about women who have had at least a modicum of independence and education. When working in social services, however, particularly in a place such as Women In Transition, one begins truly to understand the oppression of women. Part of the oppression is demonstrated as: (1) inability to identify their problems; (2) inability to articulate those problems; (3) lack of initiative; (4) lack of assertiveness; (5) deep feelings of inferiority; (6) underdevelopment of social skills; (7) underdevelopment of marketable skills; and (8) need for other-directedness.

Invariably, they have been isolated in the home and exhibit behavior patterns which are reminiscent of institutionalization.

They are fearful of travelling alone across the city. There is a very real fear of walking on the streets alone. There is a very real fear of living alone. Quite often, there is a very real fear of being alone with themselves. I would suggest these are very serious problems for women, furthermore, problems which remain unattended. An ego erosion seems to occur. Women, who at age 27, and after 10 years of sole contact with their children, themselves begin to talk in a childlike manner. I do believe the role of housewife needs serious examination. Women In Transition has a *modus operandi* which I think is very innovative and very novel, and the subject of discussion here today ultimately is alternatives. I would like to talk about alternatives.

We have reached the stage where we have to stop lamenting and sorrowing. I think if we wish to penetrate the world which is the world of men, as a social service, we must formulate and persistently define that which to date has been stated as purely emotional and concerned statements. Women have a lot of integrity. When we say there should be feminist counselling, in point of fact we are saying there should be a candidness and honesty. There should be integrity and compassion. There should be a presence of all the wonderful values which seem absent in society.

I have been very influenced by Dr. Maria Montessori in a three-fold way. (1) She was a woman; (2) She was a physician; and (3) She was very interested in education and she evolved a model. I am very touched by the kind of model she evolved because I believe that if we really and profoundly wish to help women, we must evolve a method of altering psyches. I am fascinated by the fact that it took a woman to evolve a model of education which talked of altering the field of learning.

Constantly, at women's meetings, we make reference to the female's environment. The question is, how is it formulated? Quite often we run into difficulty because, as yet, we have not learned any terms or even evolved theories around it. But I would like to say that, in the instance of Maria Montessori, and I personally employ a lot of her methods, the major thing about her style is that you alter the field of learning. It then proceeds to sharpen perception, then to stimulate individuality, and creativity. The term she used is "calling out." The term I use is "invoking." In other words, what I am trying to say is, if we want to provide services, and if we wish to help women, we have to provide contact or environments which are carefully structured, yet totally free within.

Ewa Giddings

I'm rather disappointed in the poor attendance of male doctors in the audience today. The situation reminds me of a joke I read not long ago which goes as follows: A man and woman with their drinks in their hands are meeting each other at a cocktail party. The man initiates the introduction with the statement: "I hear you're a woman doctor." The woman replies: "Well, no, I treat men as well."

This attitude appears indicative of consciousness raising in general, and in men in particular. If you are a doctor interested in issues specific to woman in our society, then you must necessarily be unable to understand or treat male clients and, most probably, you are a woman. As if information about female patients did not concern male doctors who, in fact, are the majority in this profession.

The facts, as stated this morning, show that numerous women are becoming cross-addicted as a result of doctors' negligence in detecting early signs of alcoholism in female patients, as well as a lack of awareness and set assumptions about drinking symptoms in women.

In psychotherapy jargon, we talk about helping our clients become more self-aware, more conscious of themselves and their interactions with their environment.

However, I do not know how we can possibly help others if we find it such a difficult task to raise our own consciousness and de-condition ourselves of our past stereotypic myths and beliefs. Recognition of the need, and a willingness to change, is where it starts for all of us — men, women, doctors, patients, and even organizations. An organization is a complex system of

Ms Giddings is a social worker, Clinical Institute, Addiction Research Foundation, Toronto.

individuals with different levels of consciousness. Even a more difficult task to tackle. However, an organization's willingness to look at itself and to begin to move in the direction of becoming more aware of issues being faced in society, is a great step in the right direction, in my opinion. Certainly Donwood is involved in this process. The Addiction Research Foundation is also initiating the move forward by looking at the status of their women employees. A report is in progress and should be published soon as a conjoint project of the Women Crown Employees Office regarding affirmative action programs. At present, A.R.F. is in a state of change as its mandate is moving towards being primarily one of research, with treatment occurring on a demonstrative and pilot project level. One of the projects under discussion currently is a sex role group for women.

Treatment for both sexes for alcoholism and drug addiction, at present consists of inpatient and out patient care—medical and psychotherapeutic. Out-reach and prevention are primarily handled by the branches of A.R.F., while the Clinical Institute (hospital) is involved in treatment.

Besides doing modified feminist counselling with women individually referred by the Women's Counselling Referral and Education Centre, I have the opportunity to run a wives of alcoholics group at the Alexander Park Community Centre, and Ontario Housing Project. The latter has been an especially terrific learning, and humbling, experience. I heard women share incredible stories of life struggles—eg. raising seven to nine children, looking after alcoholic husbands, keeping homes together, and working in the labor force as well. Why? Because of their conditioning and/or religious beliefs.

Where we start with this particular group of women, is where they are at, to use an overused phrase. We talk about ways to clean floors; ways to manage budget, etc. Gradually, a change of awareness occurs that they are not alone and isolated in this life, to the realization that they share a common bond. This is the *crucial* point of consciousness—change or raised consciousness. The next stage is usually one of initiating action to change their environment or circumstances.

This process is not unlike the one we as individuals and professionals, as well as organizations, need to go through in order for our consciousness to be raised. It sounds easy and is: all it takes is recognition of need, and willingness, on our part, to be open to change.

Ottie Lockey

I'm here today to represent a group of women who work collectively to staff the Women's Counselling Referral and Education Center of Toronto. I would like to return to a broader context for a moment and focus on women in society.

The title of this conference, The Chemically Dependent Woman, seems to presume that the problems of women's addiction are part of an individual pathology, and we at the Women's Counselling Referral and Education Center believe that a broad spectrum of social and political factors are responsible for the kinds of alcohol and psychotropic drug use to which women are prone. Psychotropic drug dependencies haven't materialized out of an inborn personality disorder or character defect. Women often turn to alcohol and mood-altering drugs because of their second-class status in our society. Other people here have mentioned this today, but I think it bears repeating: broad based social changes are needed in terms of abortion rights for women, the availability of contraceptive information, government-supported day care, and equal pay for work of equal value, in order for women to gain power in what remains, after 10 years of the second wave of the women's movement, a man's world.

I think Helen (Levine) spoke very eloquently about this whole area, but I would like to share with you something that happened to us at the counselling centre very recently. We were part of a demonstration in Toronto for abortion rights for women: the march took place on Saturday, May 28th. I'm sure you didn't hear anything about it. That's because the ad that we placed in The (Toronto) Star for $500 was placed in the sports section, instead of national news. I don't know how many

---

Ms Lockey is a staff member of the Women's Counselling Referral and Education Center, Toronto.

women you know read the sports section, but I don't. This, I think, demonstrates the contempt of the media for our position of defending women's abortion rights.

Treating chemically dependent women in isolation from society, allows us, as health workers, to avoid our responsibilities towards changing the attitudes and legal restrictions preventing women from fully realizing their emancipation. Chemically addicted women are, first and foremost, women and, as women, we often consider ourselves inferior to men because of the forces of social control we are exposed to from an early age — parental attitudes, teachers' expectations, cultural norms, and our own negative self-concepts. We're all too eager, often, to view ourselves as sick, to buy into a medical model, to put all the power into the hands of the nearest physician who's probably going to be a man. Since we still tend to put doctors and therapists on pedestals, the fact the doctors are male tends to contribute to the power inequity which still represents the cultural norm of a male-dominated society. The media and the pharmaceutical industry, as Ruth Cooperstock demonstrated, lead us to believe there's an instant chemical solution for every crisis, every problem, every stress-filled situation which we encounter in the course of our daily lives. After this morning, I'm sure we're all aware of the fallacy of that kind of advertising and of chemical solutions for psycho-social problems. But this afternoon's focus is: what can we provide as alternatives? Health care workers need to be aware of the resources available in the community such as the Women's Counselling Referral and Education Center in Toronto; social service agencies; vocational counselling centers like Times Change, Humber Center for Women; massage groups, exercise groups; and self-help and consciousness-raising groups.

These groups and services are available in Toronto and the Women's Counselling Center will gladly provide further information about them. As a nonsexist therapy referral service, the centre is basically interested in connecting women with appropriate therapists and therapy groups which clarify and resolve the emotional conflicts faced by individual women with addiction problems. We also stress alternatives and adjuncts to therapy, such as relaxation, exercises, yoga, nutritional considerations, and assertiveness training. Women's groups are a particularly important adjunct or alternative, especially since isolation is one of the key factors contributing to women's addiction problems. Women's groups run for, and by, women are essential to meet the special needs of women. The small group is one of the most important tools of the women's liberation movement. It has been used for consciousness raising, emotion support, and as a stepping stone towards political action.

As Cheryl Laham from CASPAR mentioned this morning, it is really important for us to come together in small groups in order to question ourselves and to answer honestly, can you respect women alcoholics? How does it feel to question a woman about her drinking? It would have been very helpful today if the structure of the seminar had incorporated the vehicle of small groups, so we might have had the opportunity to share our personal feelings about these questions with each other: I for one, am personally disappointed that I didn't have that opportunity here. As women, and as health workers, we need to meet together in small groups where all individuals may participate. I think this is a difficult format for people who may have a very valid contribution. To try and get it in five minutes at the end of a panel is really difficult. Small groups allow all individuals to participate and explore their own attitudes towards the issues under discussion; small groups provide a place where we can develop ways of providing collective support networks for those of us who are engaged in a common struggle.

In conclusion, we at the Women's Counselling Referral and Education Center, as feminists working in the mental health field, strongly believe our efforts with individual women must be accompanied by an ongoing social and political effort to alter the institutions of a society in which women still do not have control of our bodies or of our minds.

SUMMARY

It was an exciting and stimulating seminar but, not surprisingly, many questions remained unanswered at the end of it.

A chief concern voiced by participants revolved around the question of feminist counselling and how it relates to chemical dependency. The issue caused heated debate.

One speaker suggested one problem with feminist counselling may be in the term itself: people mean different things when they talk about it and this can obviously cause conflict.

Attempting to clarify the connection between feminism and alcoholism, another speaker noted that some research has shown that female alcoholics have more sex role conflicts than do male alcoholics.

Certainly, it is clear to anyone working with chemically dependent women: woman's role in society is an important factor to consider when addressing a woman's dependency problems. It seems to be a matter of timing. While the chemical dependency must be addressed directly, it is essential at the same time, that the woman be given support to alter her lifestyle so she may remain chemical free.

It is also clear that clinical research needs to be done to examine more closely the many issues surrounding chemical dependency in women.

Society changes slowly, but women are becoming more verbal and more insistent that traditional roles are not satisfactory to all of them. This is extremely thought-provoking and dissatisfaction with traditional roles may indeed be causing some chemical dependency problems in women.

The most exciting thing about the seminar was that it provided a forum for us—to share what we know about chemically dependent women, to discuss optional treatments and approaches, and to begin to think about prevention.

As women helping women, we need more forums like this one to share our feelings, shape our strategies, and increase our therapeutic effectiveness.

This was only a beginning...

Appendix A: The Program

8:30   Registration

9:00   Welcome
       Doreen Birchmore, Chairperson
       Head of Donwood Day Clinic

9:10   An Overview of the Problem
       R. Gordon Bell
       Founder and president, The Donwood Institute

9:30   Special Issues of Women in Therapy
       Susan Stephenson
       Associate Professor, Div. of Child Psychiatry
       University of British Columbia

10:00 Break

10:15 Getting in Touch with the Chemically Dependent Woman
       Lavada Pinder, Social Worker
       Director, Ottawa/Carlton Program
       of the Addiction Research Foundation

10:30 Women and Psychotropic Drug Use
       Ruth Cooperstock, Scientist
       Social Studies Dept., Addiction Research Foundation

10:45 The Chemical Trap: A Patient's Perspective
       Jean O'Brien, Health Counsellor
       The Donwood Institute

11:00 The Chemical Trap: A Physician's Perspective
       Janet L. Dowsling, Coordinator of Medical Services
       The Donwood Institute

11:15 Women Problem Drinkers: Anonymous Alcoholics
       Cheryl Laham, Community Consultant (CASPAR)
       Cambridge and Somerville Program for Alcoholism Rehabilitation
       Boston, Mass.

11:30 Dialogue and Questions

12:30 Luncheon with speaker
       Personal Reflections on Women and Alcohol
       Jan DuPlain, Executive Director (Program)
       Office on Women, National Council on Alcholism Inc.,
       Washington, D.C.

2:15   Feminist Counselling: New Directions for Women
       Helen Levine, Social Worker
       Carlton University School of Social Work
       Ottawa, Ont.

3:00   Putting the Chemically Dependent Woman in Touch with Alternatives
       Lavada Pinder: Moderator

       Lee Arima, Staff Psychologist
       The Donwood Institute

       Ann Cools, Director,
       Women in Transition

       Eva Giddings, Social Worker
       Addiction Research Foundation

       Ottie Lockey, Staff,
       Women's Counselling, Referral and Education Center
       Toronto

4:00   Summary

Appendix B: Trademark Note

These products are registered trademarks of the following companies:

Antabuse® — Ayerst Laboratories, Div. of Ayerst, McKenna & Harrison Limited

Dalmane® — Hoffmann-LaRoche Limited

Librium® — Hoffmann-LaRoche Limited

Mandrax® — Roussel (Canada) Limited

Temposil® — Lederle Products Department

Trilafon® — Schering Corporation Limited

Valium® — Hoffmann-LaRoche Limited

Vivol® — Frank W. Horner Limited

These trademarks do not necessarily represent all the trademarks under which these drugs are sold.